Why People (Don't) BUY

The GO and STOP Signals

Why People (Don't) BUY

Amitav Chakravarti
Professor of Marketing, London School of Economics, UK

Manoj Thomas
Associate Professor of Marketing, Cornell University, US

palgrave
macmillan

First published 2015 by
PALGRAVE MACMILLAN

Palgrave Macmillan in the UK is an imprint of Macmillan Publishers Limited, registered in England, company number 785998, of Houndmills, Basingstoke, Hampshire RG21 6XS.

Palgrave Macmillan in the US is a division of St Martin's Press LLC, 175 Fifth Avenue, New York, NY 10010.

Palgrave Macmillan is the global academic imprint of the above companies and has companies and representatives throughout the world.

Palgrave® and Macmillan® are registered trademarks in the United States, the United Kingdom, Europe and other countries.

ISBN 978-1-349-49987-8   ISBN 978-1-137-46669-3 (eBook)
DOI 10.1057/9781137466693

This book is printed on paper suitable for recycling and made from fully managed and sustained forest sources. Logging, pulping and manufacturing processes are expected to conform to the environmental regulations of the country of origin.

A catalogue record for this book is available from the British Library.

A catalog record for this book is available from the Library of Congress.

Typeset by MPS Limited, Chennai, India.

Contents

Acknowledgments

Many of the research results described in this book have been sourced from scientific publications. We have tried to list all the original sources of the information in the reference section. However, many scholars who are not named in this book have also contributed to the ideas expressed in this book. Our perspectives and frameworks for thinking have been influenced by our coauthors, colleagues and hundreds of brilliant students who actively participated in the debates and insightful discussions in the classes we have taught.

Details of business case studies, including direct quotes from business executives, have been sourced from the popular business press. These sources are also listed in the reference section. Although we have relied only on reputable and trustworthy publications, we cannot verify the accuracy of the details of the business case studies and the quotes from executives. Finally, please note that our characterizations of protagonists in case studies are not, in any way, meant to be evaluations of specific individuals or firms. We have used real case studies solely to illustrate the challenges encountered by managers when they try to identify and test consumer insights. Even brilliant and inspiring managers can make mistakes, and we all can learn from their mistakes.

List of Figures

List of Tables

Preface

The motivation to write this book stemmed from our frustrations in teaching consumer insights to MBA students and managers. To craft successful marketing strategies, managers have to be able to correctly predict how a marketing action will change consumer behavior.

What keeps more people from buying the product? What changes would attract more people to buy the product? Will a reduction in price make some uninterested consumers more likely to try the product? Or will it backfire and make the product look cheap? When will launching a new low-calorie pack attract non-users of the brand and when will it fail to do so? Do price cues such as discounts and coupons increase sales or do they make customers suspicious? What is the key consumer insight that will make the sales explode?

Although such predictions are the foundation of most marketing strategies, the manner in which such consumer insight questions are currently tackled vacillates between two problematic extremes. On the one hand, there is the tendency to excessively romanticize the process of generating consumer insights. Many books and managers talk about consumer insights as that elusive but magical "sweet spot" that can only be conjured up by idiosyncratically visionary business leaders or esoteric research processes. Hence the constant admonishment to "think outside the box" or "unleash one's inner creativity and insight," as well as the advocacy for esoteric research tools that promise managers that the window into the consumer's mind can only be obtained by a "dream analysis" or by analyzing the consumer's "reptilian hot-buttons."

On the other hand, there is the equally problematic tendency to fall back on simplistic surveys that rely on self-reports for generating consumer insights. For example, managers might conduct surveys that yield statements such as "60% of consumers are not happy with their current TV," or "70% of the adults surveyed love the idea of 3-D television," and use these survey results as a basis for launching into an all-out production of a "promising" new technology.

Both of these approaches are problematic. The first approach leads to wildly inconsistent results as these magical "black box" methods often don't work well when one ventures away from the product categories that they were originally tested on and found to be successful in. The magic fades away when one ventures to newer products and service categories. Additionally, they often don't hold up to scientific scrutiny. The problem with the second approach is that either (a) the "insights" derived are plain wrong (actual consumer behavior might vary significantly from self-reports), or (b) the "insights" are not actionable (e.g. even if the "70%" stat above is accepted to be true, it is not clear what kind of a 3-D television—with what kind of attributes, attribute levels and price levels, not to mention what kind of positioning and advertising—should one go about building).

Besides the problem posed by the vacillation between these two extremes, another problem is that, lamentably, none of the extant frameworks used in popular marketing textbooks—the 4Ps of marketing (product–price–place–promotion), the 3Cs of strategy (company–consumer–competition), SWOT (strength–weakness–opportunities–threat) analysis—help decision makers hone such prognoses skills.

At the same time, however, there is a wealth of research in scientific journals offering a rich repertoire of consumer behavior theories that, unfortunately, have not yet made their way into marketing textbooks. So we decided to come up with a new framework—the GO-STOP framework, the foundation of which lies in a rich tradition of scientific research—that will help managers to diagnose why consumers are not buying a product, and also help them to predict how various marketing actions would change consumer behavior. The GO-STOP framework produces actionable consumer insights.

Firms and managers are not the only entities that are interested in predicting consumer reactions accurately. Many governmental agencies and public policy entities also fret about how consumers might respond to various policy interventions such as monetary incentives, fines, public service ads, etc. The GO-STOP framework is an analytical framework that is equally useful for public policy decisions, which is something that we discuss at length in Chapters 6, 7, 8 and 9 of this book.

The GO-STOP framework is rooted in the idea that purchase decision is driven by two types of brain signals—a GO signal and a STOP signal. The GO signal energizes the consumer to approach and buy the product and the STOP signal inhibits him or her from spending money on the product. In our GO-STOP framework, it is the interplay between the GO signal and the STOP signal that determines whether or not a product is bought. If the GO signal is significantly greater than the strength of the STOP signal, then the consumer buys the product. In contrast, if the STOP signal is stronger than the GO signal, then the consumer shies away from purchasing the product. The drivers of these two signals are numerous and many of them are not readily apparent to managers, which often leads to strategic missteps.

Furthermore, the relative potencies of these two signals are influenced not only by consumers' conscious thinking but also by unconscious heuristics activated in the mind. A heuristic is a mental shortcut that people use to make quick judgments and inferences. Depending on the heuristic that consumers use, the same attribute or cue can sometimes influence the GO signal and it can sometimes influence the STOP signal. For example, a lower price can be interpreted as a "good deal," which can weaken the STOP signal and thus increase the likelihood of purchase. But it can also have an opposite effect if the lower price is interpreted as an indicator of "poor quality"; it will weaken the GO signal and reduce the likelihood of purchase. To understand and predict consumer behavior, it is important to characterize the heuristics that consumers use to make judgments and decisions, when consumers deploy which heuristics, and how such heuristic judgments influence the GO and STOP signals.

The GO-STOP framework proposed in this book offers a new perspective to marketing. It redefines the way managers should think of marketing. Effective marketing entails strengthening the GO signals and weakening the STOP signals. Successful marketers are able to identify innovative ways to strengthen GO signals and weaken STOP signals. Furthermore, successful marketers are able to correctly identify whether consumer behavior is more sensitive to GO signals or STOP signals. When consumer behavior is more sensitive to GO signals, they devise marketing strategies to strengthen the GO signal. When consumer behavior is more sensitive to STOP signals, they devise marketing strategies to weaken the STOP signal. Marketing mistakes happen when marketing actions focus on signals that consumers are not sensitive to, or when marketing actions, unintentionally, weaken the GO signal or strengthen the STOP signal.

Predicting human behavior is a complex business. For repetitive and habitual behaviors, social scientists have developed impressive models to predict future behavior. We now have quantitative models that use big data to predict behaviors with remarkable accuracy—some models can correctly predict behaviors with more than 80% accuracy. But predicting behaviors in non-repetitive and novel situations continues to be a vexing problem. It is not easy to predict the GO and STOP signals that drive consumers' behavioral responses to new stimuli—new products, new stores, new ad campaigns, etc. Of new products launched every year more than 50% fail because managers fail to correctly predict consumers' responses. In such situations, even predictions by seasoned psychologists and social scientists, more often than not, tend to be way off the mark. This fallibility of prediction necessitates testing the consumer insight predictions before formulating marketing strategies based on them. Building on the hypothesis-testing approach prevalent in the scientific literature, we suggest a new approach to market research: predict–test–learn (P-T-L). The P-T-L approach to research is quite distinct from the approach used in traditional market research.

Traditional market research managers rely on focus groups and consumer interviews as the primary research tools. In contrast, the P-T-L approach is based on the premise that even expert consumers might not have introspective access to the unconscious heuristics that influence their behaviors. Therefore, as per this approach, marketers have to come up with hypotheses (i.e. predictions) about treatments that will either strengthen the GO signal or weaken the STOP signal and then test those hypotheses using well-designed experiments. This is not a technical book on market research; however because experimental design is so fundamental to the P-T-L approach, in this book we will also discuss these concepts.

Through several case studies, we will illustrate that the GO-STOP framework is useful in explaining paradoxical consumer behavior, why smart managers and policy makers make strategic mistakes, and how to avoid such mistakes through P-T-L. In the final chapter, we propose a five-step methodology to guide the generation of actionable consumer insights. We hope that learning about the GO-STOP signals framework will change the way you think about consumer insights.

Amitav Chakravarti

Manoj Thomas

Introduction: hit-or-miss consumer insights

Behavior is context dependent

/ Improving in-store experience

Hit. In the first decade of the 21st century, Ron Johnson, a Harvard MBA, had built a formidable reputation as a brilliant retail executive. His laser-sharp focus on improving the in-store customer experience yielded rich dividends at Target. It transformed Target from just-another-discount-store to a unique store brand that sells chic yet affordable products. Target became Targé under Johnson's stewardship. Not just at Target; the same focus on customer experience during Johnson's tenure at Apple made Apple Stores, including the Genius Bar, a runaway success and one of the most profitable retail outlets in the United States. A similar focus helped him to improve patient experiences and outcomes at a Stanford University hospital.

Miss. Inexplicably, however, during Johnson's tenure at JC Penney, the same strategy led to a 25% drop in sales and over $500 million in losses in a single year—and culminated in Johnson being fired in a little over 14 months.

/ Launching a new pack

Hit. When Nabisco executives introduced the new "100-Calorie Pack" packaging format for their cookies in 2004, it was an unqualified success

and competitors rushed to copy this packaging innovation. The end result was a boom time for snack food brands with sales of 100-calorie packs of cookies reaching the $200 million a year mark by 2007, even though they often charged a 250% price premium over regular packs of cookies.

Miss. However, at the height of this 100-calorie pack frenzy in 2007, when Ocean Spray introduced a 100-calorie pack for their "Craisins" snack, it was such a failure that it was ultimately withdrawn from the market.

Bottom-of-pyramid strategies

Hit. Tata, a large multi-industry Indian conglomerate with worldwide operations, harnessed its excellent in-house engineering skills in order to reduce costs and introduce many successful innovations for bottom-of-pyramid (BOP) consumers. These innovations ranged from bringing low-cost electricity and steel to the BOP customer to providing low-cost, yet highly effective water purifiers (e.g. the "Swach" brand) and fortified energy drinks (e.g. the "Activate" and "Gluco Plus" brands). Lowering the price for the BOP consumer led to many successes for Tata and bettered the lives of many impoverished BOP consumers.

Miss. Yet, this single-minded focus on reducing the price for the BOP consumer proved to be an unequivocal failure when it came to the Tata Nano car, which, at a sticker price of $2000, was heralded by the world press as the "World's Cheapest Car" solution for the BOP consumer. Before Tata Nano, the Indian BOP consumer was stuck between the Scylla of unsafe, weather-susceptible two-wheeler driving conditions and the Charybdis of unaffordable, $4000-plus automobile prices. Tata Nano, targeted at this customer, was expected to storm the Indian market and sell hundreds of thousands of units. To put this failure in perspective, consider that a paltry 509 Nanos were sold in November 2010 (three years after its launch), at a time when automobile sales in India had reached more than 200,000 units per month.

This hit-or-miss pattern is not restricted to consumer markets; it is equally widespread in the public policy domain. There are several examples of a policy intervention leading to spectacular success in one domain, but resulting in colossal failures in other domains.

Convenience-enhancing technologies

Hit. Making it easy for consumers to order products and services from the convenience and comfort of their homes has increased consumer participation in the marketplace and led to the success of several online giants such as Amazon, eBay and Fresh Direct, to name a few.

Miss. Allowing people to cast their votes in a secure manner from the convenience of their homes completely backfired for the Swiss. Ironically, the presence of home-based (i.e. postal or online) voting significantly *reduced* voter turnout in Swiss cantonal elections from 1971 to 1999.

Monetary incentives

Hit. Governments have always used monetary carrots to encourage socially desirable behaviors. Providing monetary incentives has allowed governments all over the world to successfully encourage their citizens to buy hybrid cars, recycle plastic bottles and build energy-efficient homes, to name a few.

Miss. Monetary incentives, however, not only failed to spur blood donations, in fact they *decreased* blood donations in 2007 at the Regional Blood Center, Sahlgrenska University Hospital in Gothenburg, Sweden. Similarly, up until 2011, the UK government's sizable monetary incentive for homeowners to insulate their homes properly (in order to reduce energy waste) was not successful.

Monetary fines

Hit. In a similar vein, governments all over the world have successfully used monetary fines to curb socially undesirable behaviors such as late payment of taxes, littering and smoking in public spaces, to name a few.

Miss. Monetary fines, however, backfired when the UK government started charging its residents a small penalty for the non-recyclable trash that each household was disposing off every month. The program proved so unpopular that it had ultimately to be withdrawn. In yet another instance documented in Israel, charging parents a monetary fine for picking up their kids late from daycare actually *increased* late pickups.

Consumer insight: the fountainhead of marketing decisions

Consumer insight is the fountainhead of marketing decisions.

In 2012, two MBA students at Cornell University—Mike DeCoste and Suman Dasgupta—were enlisted to help design the marketing curriculum at their university by finding out what skills are required for a successful marketing career. They conducted a survey of marketing managers. They did not expect a conclusive answer to the question—what drives career success—as it is far too broad and nebulous a question to be conclusively answered by one study. Nevertheless, the insights generated by even attempting an answer seemed promising. So Suman and Mike began by doing one-on-one exploratory interviews with managers at middle and senior management positions.

Based on the insights from these interviews, they came up with an exhaustive list of skills that are considered relevant for marketing positions. Then they designed a survey to rank the relative importance of these skills. The survey was administered to members of several professional networks and was completed by 58 managers at different stages of their careers—associates, managers, directors and executives completed the survey. Not surprisingly, the largest representation was from marketers in the consumer packaged goods industry (41%), although other types of marketers, notably business-to-business marketers (17%) and service marketers (13%), also responded to the survey. Figure 0.1 depicts a summary of the importance ratings collected on a five-point scale.

1= Negligible Importance, 2 = Low Importance, 3 = Average Importance,
4 = High Importance, 5 = Extreme Importance

FIGURE 0.1 / **Relative importance of various skills for marketing decisions**

Source: Data from survey conducted by Cornell University MBA students, Mike DeCoste and Suman Dasgupta in 2012.

Which skills matter the most? Identifying consumer insights, along with strategic thinking and communication were the three skills that received the highest importance ratings for marketing jobs. Identifying consumer insights refers to the ability to identify new cause-and-effect patterns, behavioral patterns that consumers themselves might not be aware of, to predict consumers' response to a marketing stimulus. Strategic thinking refers to the ability to formulate a long-term product portfolio and market strategy, factoring in competitive response, to guide profit and loss forecasts. And communication refers to the ability to prioritize the right elements of a message, to use the right tone, stories, metaphors and body language to persuade internal and external stakeholders.

Although most managers believe that consumer insight is the fountainhead of marketing decisions, as the hit-or-miss vignettes in this chapter suggest, identifying consumer insights that will work in the marketplace is a challenge. Few managers can claim a very high hit rate in this area. A behavioral insight that leads to a successful marketing decision in one context can backfire and be a disaster in another context. An action designed to increase customer satisfaction can sometimes turn away the loyal customers.

Why such a disturbing pattern of hits or misses? What gives? Why does the same winning formula lead to consumer-insight home runs on some occasions and complete strikeouts at other times? There are three principal causes that have allowed this kind of a hit-or-miss pattern to persist, despite all the market research advances we have made in the last few decades. We discuss these three causes next.

chapter 1

Three causes

Why successful consumer insights are still a hit-or-miss affair

Executives often attribute marketing mistakes to a lack of customer centricity. The standard refrain is that mistakes happen because managers do not listen to the "voice of the customer." However, the problem is not so simple.

While not listening to the "voice of the customer" has often landed companies in trouble in the past, this does *not* seem to have been the case with the companies we discussed in the opening vignettes. Managers at firms such as JC Penney, Ocean Spray and Tata have always focused on the customer's unmet needs and how their actions might fulfill some of the unmet needs. No one can accuse them of not being customer-centric. Indeed, it is precisely because Ron Johnson heeded the customer's voice applauding the experience at Apple Stores, and deriding the experience at JC Penney, that he decided to make improvements to the customer experience as the centerpiece of his revival strategy for JC Penney. And it is precisely because Ratan Tata (the chief executive officer (CEO) of Tata) paid close attention to the plight of the Indian bottom-of-pyramid two-wheeler customer that he decided to embark on designing a safe, all-weather and highly affordable car for the masses. By the same token, managers at Ocean Spray had their ears on the ground with respect to the latest consumer trends and preferences, which prompted them to launch the 100-calorie packs of Craisins. So it is hard to implicate turning a deaf ear to the voice of the customer as the main reason for these customer insight errors.

We believe that these glaring mispredictions and this hit-or-miss pattern of consumer insights can be attributed to three major causes: (i) incorrect beliefs about consumer behavior, (ii) a hedgehogian approach to strategic decisions, and (iii) incorrect beliefs about market research.

A word of caution. The next few pages of this chapter might be a little too technical or concept-heavy. However, it is our sincere hope that our readers will bear with these pages. Though a bit complex, this chapter lays a critical foundation that will help readers to understand more easily why the business landscape is littered with consumer insight errors. The rest of the book will be far less technical in comparison.

First cause

Incorrect beliefs about consumer behavior

Our mental models—that is, our beliefs about how things work—shape our thought processes. The accuracy of our predictions, inferences and judgments about the world depend on the validity of our mental model of the world. If an astronomer's beliefs about the solar system are incorrect, then his predictions about the eclipse are also likely to be incorrect. If an engineer's beliefs about the properties of a material are incorrect, then his prediction about its tensile strength is also likely to be incorrect. In like vein, if a manager's beliefs about how the human mind works are incorrect, then his or her predictions about consumer behavior are also likely to be incorrect.

The mental model of consumer behavior among MBAs and managers has been influenced by economics and economists. In academia, for over a century economics has been considered the imperial social science, the noblest of all social sciences. Economists have exerted a strong influence on public policy, business strategy and business school pedagogy.

The traditional literature in economics portrays consumers as homo economicus—rational and deliberative beings always making decisions to maximize their long-term utility. As per this utility-maximization model every purchase decision is a trade-off between the utility gained from purchasing the product and the utility lost from the money that is paid to acquire the product. Consumers first assess the utility gained from the product and consider whether it exceeds the utility lost by paying the price of the product. If you were considering buying a $30,000 car, you would proceed with the transaction only if your subjective utility gained from owning the car exceeds the subjective utility lost from paying $30,000. If you are choosing among several cars, you will always choose the car that maximizes your subjective utility. Figure 1.1 summarizes the economic utility-maximization model.

At first blush, this parsimonious utility-maximization model of consumer behavior seems reasonable. Consistent with the predictions of this model, adding more attractive features to a car will make a potential customer more likely to buy the car, whereas increasing the price of the car will make him or her less likely to buy it. The utility-maximization model also yields nice—some would say beautifully precise—graphs of demand and supply. So far, so good!

However, a more careful scrutiny reveals that when it comes to predicting consumer behavior the traditional utility-maximization model and its extensions do not have much descriptive validity beyond some basic

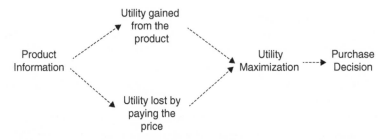

FIGURE 1.1 / The utility-maximization framework

economic transactions.[1] They are not necessarily incorrect. Rather their predictive validity is quite limited. Neoclassical economic models are useful in explaining why people are less likely to buy when price increases, and why prices tend to decrease when there is competition. But successful marketing strategies are not based on such general and obvious behavioral patterns in the marketplace. Successful marketing strategies are based on latent consumer insights that explain paradoxical consumer behaviors. When it comes to explaining why Apple is such an adored brand despite being more expensive than similar competing brands, or why consumers love "30% off" sale signs even when such signs do not mean much in an era of perpetual discounts, or why economic incentives inhibit instead of encouraging prosocial behavior, the explanations offered by traditional economic models are less persuasive.

Enter Mr Spock—the Vulcan

Traditional economic models are more prescriptive than descriptive. That is, these models do not describe actual everyday consumer behavior; instead they characterize how a "rational" consumer ought to behave. Mind you, in economics the word rationality is not used as most people use it in everyday parlance. This is rationality as defined by the mathematical models of economics. If you are a *Star Trek* fan, then think of Mr Spock, the emotionless extraterrestrial humanoid from plant Vulcan who served as the first officer aboard Captain James T. Kirk's space ship. Because he can exert complete control over his emotions and mind, and he can perform complex computations in his mind in a jiffy, Spock comes very close to economists' portrayal of a rational being.[2]

---

[1] Note that we are specifically referring to the utility maximization model of consumer behavior. When it comes to competitive strategy and macroeconomic policies, models and theories from economics continue to be the cornerstone of business school instruction. For readers more interested in the limitations of economic models of consumer behavior, please see Daniel McFadden's paper titled "The New Science of Pleasure" and other references listed for this chapter.

[2] It is intriguing that Star Trek screenwriter Gene Roddenberry did not portray Spock as a human being; he described Spock as a character from the planet Vulcan. Perhaps, he realized that human beings cannot control their emotions as Spock did.

One doesn't have to think for long to realize that ordinary earthlings do not behave like Spock. Therefore, their behaviors do not always conform to the tenets of rationality as prescribed in economics.

Here are some illustrative examples. One tenet of rationality is that a homo economicus should have consistent utility for money. For example, a rational consumer should always have more utility from $40 than from $20. So if a rational consumer finds a $20 discount attractive, then he or she should find a $40 discount even more attractive. But real-world consumers often violate this tenet of rationality. If you are like most consumers, then you would be delighted to get a $20 discount on a dress that is usually sold for $100, but would be considerably less excited by a $40 discount on an appliance that is usually sold for $2000. Although everyone knows that $40 can fetch twice the purchasing power, somehow $20 on $40 definitely seems more attractive than $40 on $2000. Clearly, consumers don't always value $40 more than $20; their valuations are influenced by somewhat arbitrary reference points in their minds.

Another tenet of rationality is that a homo economicus should have reasonably stable preferences for products. Only then can a homo economicus efficiently maximize utility. But this is seldom the case with real-world consumers. Real-world consumers' preferences for products are hugely influenced by the salient cues in their immediate environment. They learn to spontaneously respond to the cues that they have previously seen in their environment, oftentimes without even being aware of such cues. For example, consumers often use prices and brand names as cues for quality. Extensive work by branding research scholars such as Kevin Keller of Dartmouth attests to the inexorable influence of brands on consumer decision making. Brain-scanning studies have shown that the same wine actually (i.e. physiologically) tastes better when it is priced at $25 than when it is priced at $5. The same energy drink can be actually less efficacious—provide less energy—when it is sold at half the price. For Coca-Cola fans, the same cola—when served in two differently branded packs—seems tastier when it is branded as Coca-Cola than when it is branded as Pepsi-Cola. What these studies tell you is that, unlike the elusive homo economicus, real people do not have stable preferences. Consumers' preferences, and the utilities that underlie these preferences, are very labile.

Not just the subjective utility of products, even consumers' subjective valuation of money is influenced by seemingly irrational cues. Home buyers are, paradoxically, more likely to feel that they are paying a very high price for a house when it is listed as $350,000 than when it is listed as $353,465. Even though debit cards and cash are, for all practical purposes, identical modes of payment, consumers spend money more liberally when they spend using debit cards than when they spend cash. Such behavioral patterns are inconsistent with the homo economicus model of consumer behavior, suggesting that economists' model of a rational consumer might not be very useful in predicting actual consumer behavior. It is not just consumers; researchers such as Adam Alter from New York University have shown that even seasoned decision makers, such as hard-nosed stock-market investors, exhibit the same irrational patterns of behavior.

If managers and public policy formulators work with the assumption that consumers are deliberative and emotionless utility maximizers, then their predictions about consumer behavior are likely to be way off the mark. In fact, many of the consumer insight failures that we will discuss in this book can be attributed to such incorrect conceptions of consumer behavior. Real-world consumers are quick thinkers, relying on fast and frugal heuristics, and emotionally sensitive beings, intrinsically motivated to avoid negative emotions and seek positive emotions. Contrary to the view in neoclassical economics, more and more scholars now believe that the ability to think fast and emotional sensitivity are not necessarily limitations of the human mind, rather, these properties help us to adapt and thrive in new environments. Professors George Loewenstein of Carnegie Mellon and Robert Frank of Cornell University are two of those economists who have highlighted the importance of incorporating the role of emotions in economic models of decision making. They have written

extensively about this in the academic as well as popular press. However, while our quick thinking and emotional sensitivity make us the smartest species on earth, it also results in seemingly capricious and irrational behaviors. If you are in the business of predicting consumer behavior—that would include business managers, market researchers, advertisers, public policy formulators and academics—then an appreciation of the roles of heuristics and emotions is a must. Only then can you develop a more descriptive model of consumer behavior.

The GO-STOP framework: a preview

In this book, we present an alternative model of consumer behavior based on decades of research in psychology. Psychology, unlike economics, is more of a descriptive social science and does not portray humans as rational robot-like creatures. The psychological model of human behavior—the homo psychologicus—is not shackled by assumptions of rationality.

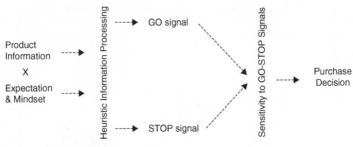

FIGURE 1.2 / **The GO-STOP framework**

Instead, psychologists understand the roles of motivational states, heuristic inferences, unconscious mental processes and emotions in adaptive human behavior. The GO-STOP framework of purchase decisions presented in this book builds on the conceptualization and empirical results documented in the cognitive, social and consumer psychology literatures. A schematic depiction of the GO-STOP framework is presented in Figure 1.2.

The GO-STOP framework is based on the premise that a purchase decision is driven by two types of brain signals—a GO signal and a STOP signal. A GO signal is a thought, feeling or an unconscious response that energizes the consumer to approach and buy the product. The STOP signal is a thought, feeling or unconscious response that inhibits him or her from spending money on the product. The GO signal activates an approach response whereas the STOP signal inhibits this response. In our GO-STOP framework, it is the interplay between the GO signal and the STOP signal that determines whether or not a product is bought. If the strength of the GO signal is significantly greater than the strength of the STOP signal, then the consumer buys the product. In contrast, if the STOP signal is stronger than the GO signal, then the consumer shies away from purchasing the product.

There are several important differences between the homo economicus model and the GO-STOP framework, which is based on psychological theories. Let us highlight the four important ones here.

First, this model postulates that *emotions play an important role in the activation and regulation of behavioral tendencies*. GO signals can be triggered by the anticipation or experience of positive emotional states (although sometimes the GO response can also be triggered by the motivation to alleviate negative emotional states). STOP signals can be activated by the anticipation or experience of negative emotional states such as the pain of parting with money or regret.

Second, the model assumes that these GO and STOP signals could either be based on *deliberative thinking* or could be triggered by *unconsciously activated heuristic rules and mental associations*. So consumers might not even be aware that some cues in the environment have activated GO or STOP signals in their brains.

Third, the model posits that the relative sensitivity to GO and STOP signals is not as invariant and stable as economists looking for tractable mathematical models would like it to be. *Relative sensitivity to cues that trigger GO and STOP signals varies across people, and even for the same person it can vary depending on the context.* Some people tend to be in a benefit-maximization mindset that makes them more sensitive to cues that trigger the GO signals (such as design, quality, prestige and taste). In contrast, some people tend to be in a pain-minimization mindset,[3] making them more sensitive to cues that trigger the STOP signal (such as unfair pricing, unhealthy ingredients and risk). Furthermore, the same person is sometimes more sensitive to GO signals (e.g. when she is buying a Hermès Birkin handbag) and sometimes more sensitive to STOP signals (e.g. when looking for the cheapest gas station in her neighborhood).

Fourth, the model stipulates that the GO and STOP signals *are not fungible*. This is in sharp contrast to the utility-maximization model, which

---

[3] Some of the technical constructs will be explained in greater detail in the subsequent chapters. Readers may refer to the glossary at the end of the book to see definitions of some of the technical concepts such as heuristics, mindsets and unconscious processing.

assumes that the utility gained from a product and the disutility (i.e. the utility lost) from paying for the product are fungible (i.e. substitutable). In other words, in the homo economicus world, there are two perfectly fungible routes to increasing the sales of a product. One could increase consumers' purchase tendencies by increasing the utility of the product (e.g. by adding new features, improving existing features). Alternatively, one could achieve the same increase in purchase tendencies by decreasing the disutility associated with paying for the product (e.g. by lowering price, offering layaway or financing plans). Either strategy should result in a very similar increase in consumers' purchase tendencies. It doesn't matter which of the two strategic options—increasing utility or lowering disutility—that managers and policy makers resort to. The economist's reasoning is very simple—after all, the impact of every intervention gets "converted" into "utilities" in the homo economicus brain, so it shouldn't matter whether we increase the utility of the product or decrease the disutility of the price. This is an erroneous assumption that often lands the utility-maximization model in trouble. The GO and STOP signal framework does not make this erroneous assumption. It does not assume that an action that increases the strength of the GO signal is interchange-able with an action that weakens the STOP signal. Quite to the contrary, the model strongly advocates "concordant" actions—a weak GO signal is best addressed by actions that strengthen the weak GO signal, not by actions that attempt to weaken the STOP signal. In a similar vein, a strong STOP signal is best countered by actions that weaken the strong STOP signal, not by actions that attempt to strengthen the GO signal. We discuss the idea of "concordance," and the perils of ignoring it, at length in Chapters 6 and 9.

The GO-STOP framework offers a new perspective on marketing. Effective marketing entails strengthening the GO signal and weakening the STOP signal. It entails identifying whether the target market is more sensitive to cues that trigger the GO signal or to cues that trigger the STOP signal, and designing product attributes and communication strategies to influence these signals.

Enough said about the GO-STOP framework for now lest we get ahead of our story. We will come back to the GO-STOP framework in greater detail in the next chapter, since, as the title suggests, it is the main focus of the book. For now, it will suffice to say that assuming incorrect models of consumer behavior (e.g. homo economicus), as opposed to the more descriptive models of consumer behavior (e.g. homo psychologicus), is a major reason why successful consumer insights remain a hit-or-miss affair.

Let us now turn our attention to the second common source of consumer insight mistakes—thinking like a rodent with quills.

Second cause

Hedgehogian thinking

Isiah Berlin, British philosopher and thinker, wrote an essay titled "The Hedgehog and the Fox" in 1953, in which he argued that influential thinkers can be divided into two categories: hedgehogs and foxes. This analogy was inspired by the ancient Greek warrior-poet Archilochus, who is reported to have noted that the fox knows many things; the hedgehog one great thing. Hedgehogs have one very effective way of dealing with adversity—they use their sharp spines or quills to protect themselves and inflict pain on their foe. When a hedgehog encounters a foe, it rolls itself into a ball such that its quills point outward. Although the purpose of comparing a hedgehog to a fox is not very obvious, Berlin used this analogy to argue that like hedgehogs, some people view the world through the lens of a single defining idea. In contrast, others, like foxes, draw on a wide variety of experiences and for them the world cannot be boiled down to a single idea.

Philip Tetlock, professor of psychology and management at the University of Pennsylvania, in a seminal 20-year-long study, compared the performance of political forecasters who had more of a "hedgehog" perspective with the performance of political forecasters who had more of a "fox" perspective. He found that despite the popularity of hedgehogs in the mainstream media, foxes tended to outperform hedgehogs in their forecasts.

He cautioned against the lure of one powerful idea that attempts to explain everything. Looking at the world through the lens of a single, albeit powerful, idea can lead to mistakes.

Tetlock's findings are very relevant for business managers. Mispredictions of consumer behavior—or incorrect consumer insights—caused by a hedgehogian view often result in misdirected business strategies. Managers often fall in love with one idea that seems powerful. They become obsessed with this seemingly powerful idea. They come to believe that this one particular idea will always beget successful marketing strategies. For example, some managers fervently believe that low prices and sales promotions are good for business. If they experience success with lowering prices and running sales promotions in one context, then they mindlessly try to implement the same strategy in all contexts without considering the fact that consumer behavior varies across contexts. A sales promotion might help a pizza delivery chain, but it might completely backfire for a formal dining restaurant. As another example, some managers adopt new packaging that is trendy because it has worked for others. So they start mindlessly adopting the new packaging in all categories. And some, like a recent *New York Times* article documented, are falling over each other to create "emporiums of cool" user experiences. Why? Because they saw some case studies suggesting that improving user experience improves financial bottom lines.

Thomas Gilovich, a renowned professor of psychology from Cornell, captures this tendency to follow the herd and oversimplify the best when he mentions in his book *How We Know What Isn't So: The Fallibility of Human Reason in Everyday Life* (1991): "People will always prefer black-and-white over shades of grey, and so there will always be the temptation to hold overly-simplified beliefs and to hold them with excessive confidence."

Instead of understanding the root cause of weak GO signals and/or intense STOP signals that afflict their product, when managers see consumer behavior through the lens of a single (often previously successful) idea they perpetuate this hit-or-miss pattern. In particular, it leads to two types of prediction mistakes that we observe in many of the examples discussed in this book: side-effect neglect and misdiagnosis.

Side-effect neglect

Side-effect neglect is a prediction error—the failure to correctly anticipate the consequences of a prescribed action. Looking at the world through the lens of a single idea can lead to side-effect neglect. In medical parlance, an effective doctor not only has to identify the intended effects of a medicine but also has to identify the unintended side effects of the medicine. If a doctor prescribes a medicine without understanding all the side effects of that medicine on various organs of the body and different types of people, it could lead to devastating outcomes. The *New York Times* discusses the case of Lloyd Balch, a 33-year-old Manhattan resident and website manager for City College of New York who was prescribed Levaquin by his doctor for fever and cough. As soon as he started taking the pill, he developed vision problems and severe pain in all his joints. He was unable to see clearly, walk uphill or climb stairs. This was obviously not the intended outcome of the prescription. Such mispredictions happen when doctors and scientists adopt a hedgehogian mindset and fail to carefully study all the possible side effects of the prescribed medicine.

In a similar vein, neglecting the side effects of a marketing action can have debilitating effects on the health of a business. If a marketing action intended to increase the GO signal inadvertently amplifies the STOP signal, it could lead to a completely unwelcome outcome. A similar misprediction can manifest when a marketing action intended to reduce the STOP signal inadvertently dampens the GO signal. We discuss several examples of such missteps in the chapters that follow.

Misdiagnosing why consumers are not buying

Again in medical parlance, misdiagnosis happens when a doctor prescribes a medicine without diagnosing the root cause of the problem. One obvious cause of misdiagnosis is laziness. For example, we know of a doctor who would unflinchingly prescribe an antibiotic to any patient who walks into his clinic with a fever. Even if the fever is caused by common cold or flu! A medical expert, quoted in the same *New York Times* article cited above, compared lazy doctors who mindlessly prescribe common antibiotics to people who are trying to kill a fly with an automatic weapon. This particular doctor's hedgehogian weapon was antibiotics.

However, laziness is not the only cause of misdiagnosis. It might not even be the most likely cause of misdiagnosis. Smart and diligent doctors can also misdiagnose a disease if environmental cues bias their reasoning. For example, if there is an outbreak of gastrointestinal illness in the area, even a smart and diligent doctor could be tempted to jump to the conclusion that a patient suffering from stomach cramps might be suffering from gastroenteritis. But if gastroenteritis is not the true cause of the stomach cramp, not only would the doctor fail to treat the root cause of the illness, but he or she might end up prescribing medicines that could actually hurt the patient.

In a similar vein, misdiagnosing the root cause of consumer behavior can lead managers to make strategic marketing mistakes. When consumers do not buy a product, it is important to understand the root cause of the behavior. Is it caused by weak GO signals? Or is it caused by intense STOP signals? The decision not to purchase a product could be because the GO signals elicited by the product are weak. We refer to such customers as *uninterested customers*. In such cases the solution should be to prescribe marketing actions that will strengthen the GO signal. Alternately, even when the GO signals elicited by a product are strong, consumers might not buy the product if the STOP signals are so intense that they completely counteract the GO signals. We refer to such customers as *conflicted customers*. In such cases the manager should prescribe marketing actions that will reduce the intensity of the STOP signals.

Misdiagnosis errors often leave managers barking up the wrong tree. They end up throwing money (in vain) at dampening the STOP signal when, in reality, the root cause of the problem lies in a weak GO signal. For example, lowering the price of a laptop is unlikely to increase sales if consumers believe that the quality is very shoddy. Alternatively, they spend a disproportionate amount of their resources trying to amplify the GO signal, when the root cause of the problem lies in a strong STOP signal. For example, offering a new flavor of a children's snack is unlikely to improve sales if most mothers are concerned about the unhealthiness of the snack. We discuss several instances of such missteps in this book.

Third cause

Incorrect beliefs about market research

The third cause of incorrect prediction is incorrect beliefs about market research. Lamentably, many managers either do not test their consumer insights or, if they do, they use incorrect methodologies to test consumer insights.

Was Steve Jobs right?

Managers often do not test consumer insights because they do not trust traditional market research. For instance, the technology marketing guru Steve Jobs is reported to have said: "Some people say, 'Give customers what they want.' But that's not my approach. Our job is to figure out what they're going to want before they do. I think Henry Ford once said, 'If I'd asked customers what they wanted, they would have told me, "A faster horse!"' People don't know what they want until you show it to them. That's why I never rely on market research. Our task is to read things that are not yet on the page." Those are some strong words from one of the legendary marketers of this century. Are his words justified? Is market research unreliable?

The honest answer is both yes and no.

In a sense, Steve Jobs was wrong.

In some situations market research can provide very reliable answers. For repetitive and habitual behaviors, the traditional market research techniques that use past behavioral data to predict future behaviors can be very reliable. In the past four decades, market researchers and academics have developed impressive models to predict repetitive and habitual behaviors of consumers using their past behaviors. For example, John Little and Peter Gaudagni of Massachusetts Institute of Technology published a paper in 1983 that is now widely acknowledged as a classic. They demonstrated that if we know (a) your grocery purchase patterns for the past six months and the prices of coffee brands in your store during this period, and (b) next week's prices and promotional schemes on all coffee brands in your regular grocery store, then we can predict with over 80% accuracy what brand of coffee you will buy on your next trip to the grocery store. Over 80% prediction accuracy—isn't that impressive?! In fact, the Nielsen research company uses behavioral data collected from retail stores to develop such models, and packaged goods giants such as Procter & Gamble, Unilever and Colgate routinely use such models to predict how consumers will react to price changes and promotional schemes. Ignoring market research in such environs would be simply foolhardy.

In another sense, Steve Jobs was right.

However, traditional market research techniques are much less reliable when it comes to behaviors in novel contexts. Powerful innovations often entail changing the status quo—putting consumers in a new retail environment, offering them a new pack that they have never seen, or offering them a new-to-the-world product. In such instances marketers don't have reliable past behavioral data to predict behavior. So it is not easy to predict how consumers will behave in such situations. For example, it is not easy to predict how many people will buy a 3-D TV using traditional research approaches. A 3-D TV entails a behavioral change—putting on a pair of 3-D glasses each time one switches on the TV. It is not easy to predict how many people will be willing to change their behavior. In a similar vein, using traditional research approaches it is not easy to predict how many people will buy the revolutionary personal transporter Segway. While we are not suggesting that market research ought to be entirely ignored in such consumption contexts, we do agree with Steve Jobs that traditional market research, as it is currently practiced, ought to be taken with a grain of salt. In fact—as we will soon describe—with three grains of salt!

Unreliable self-reports

Since past data are not available for innovative products, traditional market researchers often rely on consumer self-reports for insights and ideas, based on the premise that consumers can predict their own behavior. As depicted in Figure 1.3, they use focus groups, descriptive surveys and ethnographic studies to tap into the "voice of the customer" in the hope that such voice of the customer inputs will guide their marketing strategy.

While this does represent a lot of progress from the "production era" (up till the 1930s) or the "sales era" (up till the 1960s) when listening to the customer was largely an afterthought, for innovative products and services the traditional approach to market research is likely to lead to a haphazard hit-or-miss pattern of successes and failures. This is because of the inherent unreliability of self-reports. There is a large body of research that shows that consumer self-reports are fraught with inconsistencies and can be highly unreliable.

Several facts lay at the crux of the problem of relying on self-reports. First, consumers often do not know what they want. Second, even if consumers know what they want, they are either unaware of or simply unable to precisely articulate what are the key drivers of a purchase. Most of the problems of self-reports stem from this articulation issue. When asked whether they would like to purchase a new product or service, or when asked *why* they would like to purchase a new product or service, consumers often put on their "rational" hats and answer in terms of "shoulds" and "oughts" rather than what truly drives them. It is not a matter of intentional deception; it is just that the mere presence of an interviewer or even a research instrument such as a survey questionnaire, subtly but significantly, alters the nature of the responses that respondents provide.

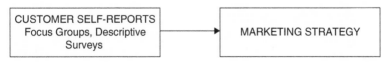

FIGURE 1.3 / Traditional approach to market research

Don't just ask, do experiment

Because research methods that rely on self-reports, such as focus groups and surveys, are inherently unreliable for innovative products and ideas, in this book we recommend an alternative approach—the predict–test–learn (P-T-L) approach. In scientific circles, this approach is often referred to as the hypothesis-testing approach. The P-T-L approach to research is quite distinct from the approach used in traditional market research.

As depicted in Figure 1.4, the P-T-L framework's first point of departure from the traditional market research approach is that it dispenses with the direct link between customer self-reports and marketing strategy. What emerges from customer self-reports should *not* be used to directly change the course of marketing strategy. Rather, the potential insights that emerge from customer self-reports should be carefully vetted through the P-T-L framework. Too often, the hit-or-miss patterns of consumer insights (such as the ones we discussed at the beginning of the Introduction), occur because managers rush to implement the voice of the customer suggestions, without vetting these suggestions through a rigorous analytical framework such as the P-T-L framework.

An important clarification is due here. Before delving into the details of the P-T-L framework, we would like to emphasize that the P-T-L

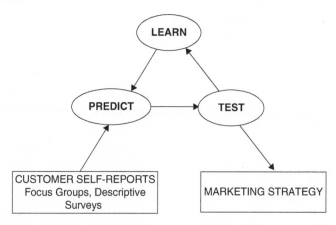

FIGURE 1.4 / **Predict–test–learn approach to market research**

framework does not suggest banishing focus groups and surveys from the research process. Rather, the exhortation is simply that self-reports from customers should be carefully *vetted* through the P-T-L framework. Focus groups and surveys are useful but only to a limited extent. Focus groups and self-reports can help to identify consumers' conscious beliefs about the factors that trigger GO and STOP signals. But these beliefs might not be accurate. And, more importantly, focus groups and surveys will not reveal innovative ways to strengthen the GO signal or weaken the STOP signal.

A similar clarification is also due for our earlier criticism of the hedgehogian manager who relies too much on his or her past experiences. Our criticism of the hedgehogian manager should not be misinterpreted as a call to cast aside all past experiences. These can be useful *provided* they are carefully vetted through the P-T-L process. In short, while we disapprove of hedgehogian managers who do not test, we believe that hedgehogian managers who religiously practice the P-T-L process can be great consumer insight champions. Blindly implementing learnings from past experiences is a recipe for disaster or, at best, a wild gamble. However, relying on past learnings to generate insightful ideas, and then testing them, could be a path to success.

Predict–test–learn and then predict again

The first step in the P-T-L framework is to *generate testable predictions*.

Testable predictions entail two elements—a proposed change (scientists refer to this as the *treatment or the independent variable*) and the effect of that change on consumer behavior (scientists refer to this as the *outcome or the dependent variable*). Testable predictions are often more meaningful when you have two or more of them based on *competing* insights. Here is an example of two predictions for an orange juice brand based on very distinct consumer insights:

Prediction 1: if we reduce our price to attract price-sensitive customers (treatment variable), then our overall sales will improve by 5% (outcome variable).

Prediction 2: if we increase the frequency of consumption of our regular customers by introducing a smaller single-serve pack (treatment variable), then our overall sales will improve by 5% (outcome variable).

In order to generate testable predictions, managers have several sources of input at their disposal. The self-reports from customers, gathered through surveys and focus groups, is one such source. Testable predictions can also be generated by looking at the prevailing wisdom or the latest thinking among industry experts. Predictions can also be generated by extrapolating emerging trends from similar industries and markets. Another very important source, one that is often neglected by practitioners, is basic research in social sciences such as psychology, behavioral economics, sociology and anthropology.

The second step in the P-T-L framework is to *test the predictions via carefully designed experiments*.

Several decades ago the advertising guru David Ogilvy said: "The most important word in the vocabulary of advertising is TEST. If you pretest your product with consumers, and pretest your advertising, you will do well in the marketplace." Ogilvy's philosophy is as relevant today as it was in the 20th century. We would like to emphasize here that focus groups and descriptive surveys do not qualify as testing techniques. Testing requires *well-designed experiments*. It is important that the predictions that emerge from the first stage of the P-T-L process are tested using carefully designed experiments as opposed to other forms of research that rely on self-reports. Experiments, also referred to as randomized control trials (RCTs), split testing, or A/B testing, are a superior testing tool primarily because of their unique ability to establish causality (as opposed to mere correlation).

The third step in the P-T-L framework is to *learn from the results of the testing phase*.

The main task of this phase is to analyze the outcomes that were measured and determine whether or not the predictions from the second stage hold true. This primarily involves comparing the experiment group to the control group and looking for statistically significant (and practically meaningful) differences on the measured outcomes. It is important to understand that there is learning even if the predictions "fail" as it probably indicates that the key intervention is not effective, thus freeing up managers to pursue other more efficacious interventions. Burt Rutan, an American aerospace engineer noted for his originality in designing innovative aircrafts, is reported to have said: "Testing leads to failure, and failure leads to understanding." In a similar vein, Jeff Bezos, the founder of Amazon, is reported to have said: "Invention requires experimentation and experimentation implies failure. If you know it's going to work, then it's not an experiment."

In order for a richer learning at this stage it is important to understand why an intervention succeeded or failed. This requires collecting and analyzing "process measures" along with the key outcomes. Process measures refer to variables that shed light on the thought process of the study participants (e.g. their perceptions of orange juice on different dimensions such as expensiveness, healthfulness, quality and taste), as opposed to the ultimate outcomes alone (e.g. the predicted 5% increase in overall sales). The analysis of the process measures might help in understanding why an intervention did not work, whether certain changes might lead to more effective interventions, or even developing new predictions and hypotheses.

Finally, it is always good practice to collect and analyze some additional "segmentation"-related data (e.g. age, gender, income, socioeconomic status or other individual-level variables) because sometimes the analysis might reveal that the intervention is more effective among certain subgroups of the sample (e.g. families with children versus families without children). The analysis of differential effectiveness of the intervention among different subgroups of the sample can also help to inform future research efforts. For a brief but insightful look into the world of experiments, readers are referred to two excellent articles by Dan Ariely (Duke

University), Eric Anderson (Northwestern) and Duncan Simester (MIT). Ariely talks about why, despite the usefulness of experiments, many firms continue to resist implementing them, and Anderson and Simester provide excellent tips on conducting experiments in business settings. The reference section for this chapter provides the details of these two articles.

GO-STOP framework, P-T-L and the structure of the book

In the rest of the book we discuss several recent examples of consumer insight missteps and how a rigorous P-T-L vetting process could have helped in avoiding these missteps. To get the P-T-L process off to a good start, it is important to come up with good predictions at the predict stage. As we mentioned earlier, customer self-reports, opinions of industry experts, the prevailing wisdom in an industry and battle-tested theories from the basic sciences, to name a few, can act as sources of input for the predict stage. The GO-STOP framework that we present in this book can help to unify the inputs from these different sources and come up with coherent predictions. The GO-STOP framework is a useful tool for managers to structure their thinking and their discussions, and also to present their rationale to stakeholders. It can help to explain paradoxical consumer behavior (like the hit-or-miss examples we described at the beginning of the Introduction), understand why smart managers and policy makers commit strategic mistakes, and provides an analytical toolkit for avoiding such mistakes. We discuss the GO-STOP framework in more detail in Chapter 2.

chapter 2

The 100 calories paradox
An insightful packaging innovation

Jennifer's dilemma

Keebler's deluxe chocolate chip cookies are Jennifer's favorite brand of cookies. They are neither too chewy nor too crumbly. And they have just the right amount of chocolate chips in them to make them irresistible. So on a Saturday evening in 2004, during a weekly visit to the grocery store when she found that Keebler's deluxe chocolate chip cookies were on sale—two regular packs for $5—she was instinctively inclined to add two packs to her shopping cart.

But something held her back. Each regular pack contained 14.2 oz of cookies. Is it wise to have two large packs of the sugar-and-carbohydrates-filled vice in her pantry? She wondered. Two large packs of chocolate chip cookies would surely put her self-control to test. She knew that if she had a pack of cookies sitting around, she would be tempted to grab one whenever she is in the kitchen. The temptation would be particularly difficult to overcome when she is hungry or tired. As she was mulling over this dilemma, her eyes fell on the 100-calorie packs of the same brand of cookies on the adjacent shelf. Luckily for her, the 100-calorie packs were also on sale that week—two 100-calorie packs for $5. Instead of two regular packs, she could buy two 100-calorie packs for the same amount

REGULAR PACK
500 calories for $5

DIET PACK
100 Calories for $5

The Price of Making an Indulgence Justifiable

of money. Each 100-calorie pack contained 4.44 oz of cookies and they were divided into six single-serve pouches. This certainly is a more justifiable way to indulge my cravings, thought Jennifer as she walked to the checkout counter with the two 100-calorie packs in her shopping cart.

Jennifer is one of the millions of cookie lovers who have switched from regular packs to 100-calorie packs. The concept of the 100-calorie pack—which offers about one-third less product for the same price—was introduced in 2004 by Nabisco and has been a remarkable success in the snack food industry. In 2004, there were about five brands of 100-calorie packs available on the market. Within a year this number was closer to 50 with several other major food brands launching their own version of 100-calorie packs. In 2014 practically every major food brand has a 100-calorie version of their product available in the market. Pepperidge Farm started selling 100-calorie variations of Goldfish and other cookies. Potato wafers and beef

TABLE 2.1   Price premiums paid for 100-calorie packs

Product	Percentage Increase in the Price of 100-Calorie Pack Versions
Cheese Nips	279%
Keebler Chips Deluxe Cookies	250%
Chex Mix	248%
Ritz Crackers/Snack Mix	229%
Goldfish Pretzels	196%
Keebler Graham Crackers	188%
Oreo Cookies/Thin Crisps	187%
Keebler Sandies Cookies	185%
Snyder's Pretzels	175%
Chips Ahoy Cookies/Thin Crisps	175%
Goldfish Crackers	167%
Pringles	163%

Source: Data from Centre for Science in the Public Interest report on 100-calorie prices available at http://cspinet.org/new/200708141.html (accessed 2 November 2014).

jerky were offered in 100-calorie packs. Sales of 100-calorie packs reached $200 million annually after just three years on the market.

The success of the 100-calorie packs is baffling when one compares the unit prices of these packs with the unit prices of regular packs. Consumers who purchase these packs are paying double the unit price, and sometimes triple the unit price, relative to the regular packs. The Centre for Science in the Public Interest, the publisher of Nutrition Action Healthletter, recently did a study of the "premium" that consumers pay for the 100-calorie versions. For some of the popular brands such as Cheese Nips, Keebler Chips and Chex Mix, consumers are paying as much as 250% more for the 100-calorie pack versions. The results from their price comparisons study are summarized in Table 2.1.

Even retail executives were surprised by the success of 100-calorie packs. Their experience suggested that a typical consumer is sensitive to the prices of discretionary food products. Their experience also told them that a small increase in price substantially reduces the sales of discretionary food items such as cookies, crackers, sugar confectionery and soft drinks. Therefore, they predicted that consumers would be unwilling to pay for what one executive called discretionary food products that are "overpriced and under-filled." But quite to the contrary, the 100-calorie pack has emerged to be one of the most successful packaging innovations in the food industry.

100 calories everywhere, but...

By 2007 the 100-calorie pack innovation initiated by Nabisco had reached a frenzy point with practically every food manufacturer joining the band-wagon. All major food brands—Cheese Nips, Keebler Chips, Chex Mix, Oreo, Pringles—had come out with a 100-calorie version of their product. Perhaps it is this frenzy that nudged Ocean Spray to launch 100-calorie packs of craisins. Ocean Spray, an agricultural cooperative of growers of cranberry and grapefruit, sells several healthful and natural products such as cranberry sauce, fruit juice and health snacks. The cooperative has introduced several innovative cranberry-based products, craisins being one of them. Craisins are dried cranberries made by drying fresh cranberries, a process similar to mak-ing grapes into raisins. Ocean Spray played a major role in popularizing the use of craisins in trail mix, salads, cereals, or simply to be eaten on their own. In fact "Craisin" is a registered trademark of Ocean Spray Cranberries, Inc.

Keen to position craisins as a healthy snack, Ocean Spray managers decided to participate in the 100-calorie frenzy. In 2007, they launched a 100-calorie craisins pack that consisted of an outer pouch with six individually wrapped 1 oz pouches. Each 1 oz pouch contained enough craisins to comprise 100 calories. Although the distribution of this new pack had reached its peak in two years, sales of this 100-calorie pack were disappointingly low. The managers were stumped.

Paradoxical behavior

Both events, the resounding success of the 100-calorie cookies and the colossal failure of 100-calorie craisins, raise very interesting questions about underlying consumer behavior. First consider the success of 100-calorie cookies. Why are otherwise price-sensitive consumers willing to pay such a premium for portion control? What psychological mechanisms underlie such consumer behavior? Now consider the failure of 100-calorie craisins. Why weren't consumers buying 100-calorie packs of craisins yet they were happily gobbling down 100-calorie packs of cookies? Delineating the GO and STOP signals in both these cases can help us to unravel this conundrum.

Back to GO and STOP signals

The success of the 100-calorie pack is a fascinating case study on consumer insights. It offers a good illustration of the GO-STOP framework that we introduced in Chapter 1. As we discussed in Chapter 1, the drivers of any purchase decision can be numerous and varied. These drivers might act independently, complementarily, or in opposition to each other. To complicate matters further, marketing actions such as advertising and pricing changes might interact with these drivers. It is this complex set of influences that determines whether a consumer will purchase a product or a service, or forgo it. The multitude and variety of decision drivers notwithstanding, we believe that the essence of many purchase decisions can be distilled down to two fundamental and often opposing drivers: a GO signal that motivates the consumer to approach and buy the product and a STOP signal that inhibits him or her from spending money on the product. Let us understand these two types of signals and the environmental cues that trigger them.

The GO signal is a thought, feeling or an unconscious response that energizes the potential buyers toward the product. It comprises all the signals that *attract* the potential buyer toward the product or service in question. It is what drives the potential buyer's motivation to consume the product or service. The GO signal, if not inhibited by the STOP signal, will result in a purchase. Most obviously, the quality of the product or the key differentiating product attributes can trigger and strengthen the GO signal. However, it is important to note that several other less obvious aspects of the purchase or consumption process could also drive the GO signal.

For example, design, packaging and brand name could trigger GO signals (think of iPhones or iPads). Other aspects of the consumption journey such as the in-store experience, interactions with salespeople, after sales service, social signaling value (i.e. how highly one is perceived by others on being seen using the product) and self-signaling value (i.e. how highly one is perceived in one's own eyes on using the product), to name a few, can also serve as important triggers of the GO signal.

In contrast, the STOP signal is a thought, feeling or an unconscious response that inhibits the purchase decision. It comprises all the signals that *repel* or *hold back* the potential buyer from the product or service in question. A STOP signal can manifest in several forms—the pain of paying, anticipated regret, perceived risk, the feeling of uncertainty—all of which can counteract the urge to buy. STOP signals can override the GO signal and prevent potential buyers from purchasing the product. The most obvious driver of the STOP signal is the price of the product. A high price, in some circumstances, could cause "pain of paying" and thus counteract the GO signals. However, here too, it is very important to think of the other, less obvious aspects of the consumption experience that might be acting as brakes and keeping the consumer away from the product. For example, the feeling of guilt ("It looks delicious but I feel guilty eating a cookie!") and justifiability ("I cannot justify paying that much for a pencil!"), concerns about the in-store experience ("Too cluttered!"), unpleasant interactions with salespeople ("Too pushy!"), after sales service ("Too little!"), social signaling value ("Does it signal low status to others?"), and self-signaling value ("Does it contradict the kind of a person I see myself as?"), to name a few, could easily act as drivers of the STOP signal. As an aside, note that since consumer self-reports can be unreliable, on some occasions a GO signal might masquerade as a STOP signal (or vice versa). We discuss how to deal with this potential problem in Chapter 10.

In our GO-STOP framework, it is the interplay between the GO signal and the STOP signal that determines whether or not a product gets bought. If the strength of the GO signal is significantly greater than the strength of the STOP signal, then the consumer buys the product. In contrast, if the STOP signal is stronger than the GO signal, then the consumer shies away from purchasing the product. If the two signals are roughly equal in strength, then the decision becomes very vulnerable to even the slightest of changes in the relative strength of the GO and STOP signals.

Effective marketing thus entails using consumer insights to strengthen the GO signal and weaken the STOP signal. Effective marketers know when to focus on cues that trigger GO signals and when to focus on cues that weaken STOP signals. When their targeted customer's behavior is more sensitive to the GO signal, they devise marketing strategies to strengthen the GO signal. When their targeted customer's behavior is more sensitive to the STOP signal, they devise marketing strategies to weaken the STOP signal. Successful marketers are able to correctly identify whether consumer behavior is more sensitive to the GO signal cues or to the STOP signal cues. The case study of the 100-calorie pack is an excellent example of influencing consumer behavior by weakening the STOP signal.

Let us see how the GO-STOP framework can help us to understand Jennifer's 100-calorie-pack cookie purchase decision. As illustrated in Figure 2.1, when Jennifer was standing before the regular pack of cookies, she was pulled in different directions by the GO and STOP signals in her mind. On the one hand, her intrinsic liking for chocolate chip cookies might have triggered visceral responses—such as salivation and hunger—motivating her to buy the regular pack of cookies. On the other hand, the anticipation of the post-consumption regret and guilt, and the likely negative feelings caused by thinking about an expansion of her waistline, would have triggered the STOP signal, inhibiting her purchase motivation. It is this state of dilemma caused by two conflicting signals, one driving her toward the purchase decision and the other inhibiting her purchase decision, that made the 100-calorie pack seem particularly appealing to her. The 100-calorie pack enabled her to track her calories and helped her to restrict her consumption to 100 calories in one sitting. This feature of the packaging innovation significantly reduced the strength of the STOP signal that was inhibiting her purchase of the regular pack. The 100-calorie pack was less likely to make her feel guilty about consuming cookies. Thus, the weakening of the STOP signal by significantly reducing the feelings of guilt that were driving the STOP signal, facilitated a purchase decision in this case.

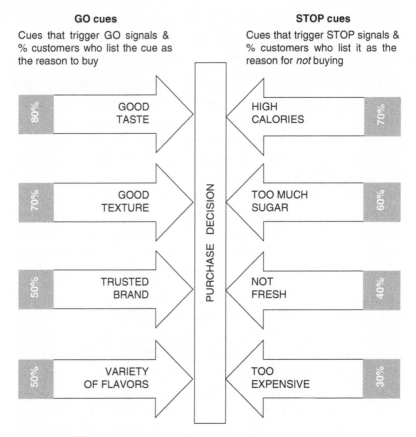

FIGURE 2.1 / GO and STOP signals for Keebler cookies

/ Why not 100-calorie craisins?

To answer this question we have to first understand whether consumers'
reluctance to purchase craisins was caused by a weak GO signal or a strong
STOP signal. The 100-calorie packaging was effective in increasing the
sales of cookies, chips and other indulgent food items because in these
product categories it was a strong STOP signal that was preventing
potential consumers from buying. The 100-calorie packaging appealed
to reluctant consumers who had a visceral craving for cookies, but were

reluctant to buy cookies because of the perceived unhealthiness of the consumption: "I am so tempted to eat these cookies, but I cannot because they are unhealthy." For such customers, the 100-calorie pack was a very appealing alternative to the regular pack because by reducing portion size—by making the cookies smaller and by packing them in smaller packs—the marketer reduced the consumption guilt without in any way reducing the visceral appeal of the cookies. Said differently, the packaging innovation weakened the STOP signal that was inhibiting the purchase. This is why the 100-calorie pack boosted cookie purchases.

There are two powerful consumer insights behind the success of 100-calorie cookies. First, the marketers at Nabisco understood that there are a significant number of their customers who are more sensitive to STOP signals caused by health concerns. Trying to win them over by enhancing the GO signals—for example by offering more delicious cookies or by offering organic cookies—would not work because their behavior is more sensitive to STOP signals than to GO signals. Second, these marketers identified a powerful packaging innovation to weaken the STOP signal. Offering a packaging that restricted consumption to just 100 calories was the perfect antidote to the anxiety caused by health concerns.

Craisins purchases, in contrast, were not inhibited by a strong STOP signal. Consumers had no qualms in buying dried cranberries—because they were neither unhealthy nor too expensive. Rather, the reluctance to purchase craisins was caused by a weak GO signal. Potential consumers did not find craisins appealing enough to begin with. Some found craisins to be too tart. Other considered dried cranberries, like prunes, a health food rather than a hedonic snack. Unlike cookies and crispy potato chips, craisins did not cause salivation or other visceral responses associated with desire. Given this background, is it surprising that a tactic designed to weaken the STOP signal did not have any noticeable effect on consumer behavior? We think not.

Instead of blindly adopting a tactic designed to weaken the STOP signal, Ocean Spray managers should have focused on a strategy to strengthen the GO signal elicited by craisins. Launching 100-calorie craisins, in our opinion, was a clear case of a very competent and successful marketer adopting a trendy marketing strategy without diagnosing the root cause of consumer behavior. An error that, perhaps, could have been avoided if the marketer had relied on the GO-STOP framework to identify why consumers are not buying craisins.

Standing on the shoulders of giants

The GO-STOP framework that we present in this book is not a fanciful framework that we came upon on the spur of the moment. It is rooted in a rich and diverse literature. We stand on the shoulders of giants. The notion that behavior is influenced by two opposing forces, one that propels action and the other that restrains action, has been discussed and debated by philosophers and psychologists for centuries. The Greek philosophers Plato and Socrates debated whether it is wiser to secure pleasure or to avoid pain. Jeremy Bentham, the British philosopher, argued that "Nature has placed mankind under the governance of two sovereign masters, pain and pleasure." Kurt Lewin, a German-American psychologist who held faculty positions at Cornell and MIT, came up with a framework to study the different forces that make up the totality of the situation, called force field analysis, which looks at forces that are either driving movement toward a goal (helping forces) or blocking movement toward a goal (hindering forces).

Several other psychologists and behavioral scientists have argued that appetitive motivational systems promote approach behaviors that seek a reward or positive outcome, whereas aversive motivational systems promote avoidant behaviors that seek to avoid punishment or a negative outcome. Jeffrey Alan Gray, a British psychologist, proposed that behavior is controlled by two systems, the behavioral inhibition system (BIS) and the behavioral activation system (BAS). The BIS makes people sensitive to pain and triggers avoidance motivation, while the BAS makes people sensitive to rewards and triggers approach motivation. Charles Carver and Teri White developed self-report scales to measure individuals' personality related dispositional BAS and BIS sensitivities. Tory Higgins, a professor of psychology at Columbia University, developed regulatory focus theory arguing that people pursue their goals using two separate regulatory orientations—promotion orientation and prevention orientation. Promotion-oriented individuals tend to maximize gains and are more sensitive to the presence or absence of positive outcomes. Prevention-oriented individuals seek to minimize losses and are more sensitive to the presence or absence of negative outcomes. Such basic approach and avoidance tendencies have also been successfully used in understanding the processes that lead to maladaptive behaviors, as such behaviors (e.g. impulsivity, suicide, fighting, alcohol, marijuana and other drug abuse) are often characterized by a constant battle between approach and avoidance tendencies.

Scholars working on animal learning theories have argued that not just human beings, but other organisms, are also innately wired to maximize pleasure and minimize pain. Such instinctive approach–avoidance responses have been documented in rats, mice, birds, cats, dogs and cows. Even unicellular organisms such as amoeba exhibit approach and avoidance tendencies toward the stimuli they encounter in their environment. For example, some researchers have documented that a weak light stimulates a local flow of protoplasm toward the light while an intense light makes it move away from the light. The fact that even unicellular organisms incapable of logical reasoning and rational thinking can be influenced by GO and STOP signals suggest that logical reasoning and rational thinking is not necessary for the GO and STOP signals to manifest in the brain. GO and STOP signals can be instinctive or reflexive responses learned from prior experiences.

Fast and frugal thinking

Let us go back to Jennifer's purchase decision once again and probe deeper into her thought process while she was buying the 100-calorie pack. The 100-calorie packaging reduced the intensity of the STOP signal relative to the regular pack because she found it easier to justify the purchase of a 100-calorie pack than to justify the purchase of a regular pack of cookies. But is paying almost 300% more for the 100-calorie pack really justifiable? If we were to intercept Jennifer in the store and ask her to justify why she is spending almost 300% more for portion control, would she be able to offer a coherent and logical justification? Our guess, informed by our knowledge of consumer behavior, is that she might not be able to do so. In fact, when confronted with such a question, she might even be a bit surprised by her own decision. She might say, "Hmm… I don't know why, but I somehow did not feel bad about paying almost 300% more for the 100-calorie packs."

This observation highlights an important aspect of the GO-STOP framework: the judgments and inferences that trigger the GO and STOP signal are not always based on conscious thinking. The GO and STOP signals can be activated, amplified or dampened by unconscious heuristics that guide our everyday judgments and inferences.

What is a heuristic?

Heuristics are simple, efficient rules that enable us to make quick decisions. Heuristics can be learned through prior experience or acquired through evolutionary processes. Heuristic decision making is fast and frugal and is often based on the evaluation of one or two salient bits of information. We use heuristics, sometimes consciously and sometimes unconsciously, to efficiently navigate through the complex maze of everyday decisions. Nobel laureate Daniel Kahneman in his book *Thinking, Fast and Slow* (2011) defines a heuristic as a "simple procedure that helps find adequate, though often imperfect, answers to difficult questions." Gerd Gigerenzer and Wolfgang Gaissmaier of the Max Planck Institute of Human Development, Berlin, offer the following definition of a heuristic: "A heuristic is a strategy that ignores part of the information, with the goal of making decisions more quickly, frugally, and/or accurately than complex methods."

The GO and STOP signals that influence consumers' purchase decisions can be influenced by such heuristic evaluation of information. Jennifer seemed to have ignored the steep price increase because the aversive feeling, the STOP signal that was inhibiting her purchase decision, was not based on a systematic trade-off analysis between calories and price. Standing in front of the cookie aisle she was not deliberating on what would be a reasonable price for the additional convenience offered by smaller packaging. Instead the STOP signal was based on a heuristic that "high-calorie food is bad and cookies are high-calorie food." If the STOP signal is caused primarily by the aversive response to calorie content of the product, then framing the product as low in calories is an ingenious way to weaken the aversive response. The 100-calorie pack was an ingenious way to weaken the STOP signal. It is a brilliant innovation based on a rich consumer insight. It triggered the heuristic inference: "This is not a high-calorie pack, so I can buy it without guilt."

Once the STOP signal was weakened and the tension caused by the conflicting forces of the STOP and GO signals was relieved, Jennifer did not care much about the price. The fact that the smaller packs were priced almost three times more than the regular packs did not matter much. Indeed, as some studies have shown, the relief from resolving this tension not only prompts Jennifer to ignore price, but it also leads her to lower her guard and, ironically, consume more calories.

Don't just ask, do experiment

Let us turn back the clock to 2003, the year preceding the launch of the 100-calorie pack in the market. Imagine that the 100-calorie pack is still in the concept development stage. That is, it has not been launched yet. And imagine that you are the manager at Nabisco entrusted with the task of developing the pricing strategy for the 100-calorie pack. Your mandate is to find out how much of a price premium consumers would be willing to pay for the 100-calorie pack. You hire a reputed market research agency to help you arrive at the optimal price. The agency proposes the following research plan: conduct a few focus groups followed by a survey to measure consumer willingness to pay (researchers abbreviate this as WTP) for the 100-calorie pack.

Focus groups are perhaps the most popular form of qualitative research in marketing, wherein a group of potential consumers are asked about their perceptions and attitudes toward a new concept or idea. A typical focus group is conducted in an interactive group setting; the moderator asks a question and then all participants share their responses to the question. Participants are also free to talk with other members participating in the focus group. After getting an initial sense of the WTPs through focus groups, the agency proposes to confirm the WTP through a quantitative survey.

How would you respond to this proposal? Do you think any participant in the focus group or respondents to a survey would acknowledge that they are willing to pay a 300% price premium for the 100-calorie pack? Our view, as discussed in the P-T-L approach in Chapter 1, is that focus groups and WTP surveys that rely on self-reports from consumers are not very useful in this situation. If you ask potential consumers to indicate the premium that they are willing to pay for the 100-calorie pack, it is very unlikely that they will say they are willing to pay a 300% premium for a packaging innovation. Asking potential consumers direct questions about price is likely to alter their evaluation of price. Direct questions make them focus on price as a standalone or focal variable. This, in turn, changes the heuristics or decision rules that they use to evaluate price compared to what they naturally use in the store while making the actual shopping decision.

The act of measuring changes what is being measured.

Asking consumers about their willingness to pay might, for example, make them focus on the fairness of the pricing strategy. Should the price of conveniently packaging cookies be more than that of the cookies itself? The most likely answer would be negative. After all, transforming a regular pack to a 100-calorie pack is not a daunting task. *You could actually do it in your own kitchen.* All that you need is a few small Ziploc-type resealable plastic bags. If the cost of making a pack of cookies is $2.50, it just seems unreasonable and unjustifiable to pay more than 50 cents, or $1 at the most, for more convenient packaging.

This discussion takes us back to an important mantra from the P-T-L framework that we discussed in Chapter 1: *don't just ask, do experiment*. Asking consumers about their willingness to pay, or asking them why they buy or don't buy a product, could lead to misleading information. The questions that the researchers ask could change the spotlight of consumer attention from the GO signal to the STOP signal or vice versa. Researchers' questions could also change the heuristics that they use to process the information. So instead of asking direct questions about a particular behavioral insight, it is better to test the insight through well-designed *experiments* or *randomized control trials* (RCTs). If you want to test whether consumers are willing to pay 100%, 200% or 300% more for 100-calorie packs, it is best to run an experiment with four different conditions: a control condition and three treatment conditions. In the control condition the new pack would be priced at the same level as the regular pack, in the other three conditions the new pack would be priced at 100%, 200% and 300% higher levels, respectively. Participants would be randomly assigned to any one of these conditions and participants in any condition would not be aware of the existence of the other conditions. Then we can compare actual purchases or stated purchase intentions across the four conditions in order to study how consumers respond to different price levels of the 100-calorie packs. Results from such experiments are likely to be much more diagnostic than directly asking consumers in focus groups and WTP surveys.

The act of measuring changes what is being measured

Such experiments could be conducted in the field (field experiments) or they could be conducted in a laboratory (laboratory experiments) on a smaller scale. Field experiments offer greater external validity; the results are likely to be closer to actual consumer behavior. Laboratory experiments, in contrast, offer greater internal validity. Laboratory experiments can be done in more controlled settings, enabling researchers to clearly delineate the mechanism underlying the effect. In this book, we will present the results from several fascinating field and laboratory experiments on consumer insights.

Having described the basic nature of the GO-STOP framework, in the following chapters we look at some glaring pricing mistakes that were caused by incorrect consumer insights. Knowing the basic workings of the GO-STOP framework will be important in understanding (and avoiding) these pricing mistakes, as these mistakes stem from a poor understanding of the GO and STOP signals associated with the company's product or service.

3

Pricing disaster at JC Penney

Know how your price cues operate

Early in 2011, JC Penney, or Penney's as it is commonly referred to, continued to be besieged by lackluster sales figures. Its revenues and profits in 2011 were lower than they were 15 years earlier, and it suffered a 5% drop in revenue from 2010, to $5.43 billion (while its rival, Macy's, saw an increase of 5.5%, to $8.72 billion), and a net income loss of $87 million. Despite its 111-year storied history, in recent years the brand continued to decline. According to retail experts, at the core of these disheartening figures was a trifecta of problems that revolved around JC Penney's brand image, in-store consumer experience and pricing strategy.

JC Penney's brand image was outdated. It was regarded as a dowdy brand aimed at the middle class (when the middle class itself was in peril in America), and shoppers were reluctant to visit the stores of a faded brand. It also didn't help matters that JC Penney's in-store consumer experience was chaotic. A journalist visiting its Palisades Center in New Jersey reported dirty floors, clothes unfolded and strewn all around and items such as cheap jewelry and toys lying in the middle of aisles in their half-opened containers.

To overcome the twin hurdles of a fading brand image and a chaotic shopping environment, both of which deterred store traffic, JC Penney had become increasingly reliant on a "bargain hunt" pricing strategy to lure shoppers through the door. In 2011 alone the company ran a mind-numbing 590 promotions, with 72% of its wares being sold at discounts of 50% or more and only 0.2% of sales being made at full price. This pricing strategy comprising endless rounds of special sales, discounts and coupons was beginning to have at least three detrimental knock-on effects. First, effectively, JC Penney's list prices were largely fictional, a fact that was not lost on its consumers, who happily cherry-picked between JC Penney's own promotions and those of competing stores such as Macy's. Second, this maze of pricing promotions and special deals was beginning to confuse its consumers and especially annoy its coupon-weary consumers. Third, and perhaps most importantly, JC Penney appeared to be trapped in an ever-deepening spiral of special deals, with each passing year requiring deeper and deeper discounts in order to drive sales. A vicious cycle appeared to have set in. The heavy discounts contributed to the in-store mess that was commonly reported, and this in-store mess led to a poor in-store consumer experience, which in turn, could only be overcome by luring consumers with an even deeper discount.

The perfect solution: a retail star

By any measure of success, Ron Johnson is a veritable retail star. After graduating from Stanford University and briefly working in accounting he went on to Harvard for his MBA. Unlike most of his peers at Harvard, he turned down lucrative offers from top Wall Street investment banks to work instead in a mid-tier, Midwestern retail chain, Mervyn's. In explaining his seemingly unusual choice, Johnson stressed the importance of learning the retail business from the ground up: "I want to run a company one day, and I need to learn the business from the ground up." He further commented, "I thought, I want to be really good at something."

And boy was he really good at it!

Johnson is widely credited with hatching two of the most successful retail concepts in a generation. First at Target, from 1990 till 1999, his designer initiatives such as the Michael Graves line of products were such a smash hit that they changed Target's image from being just-another-discount-store to one of a unique store brand that sells chic yet affordable products. Then at Apple, Johnson continued to weave his retail magic during his tenure there from 1999 till 2011. At Apple he worked with Steve Jobs to create the now familiar, sleek and gleaming Apple Stores that we are so enamored with. Johnson's original ideas, though often at odds with the famously outspoken Jobs (e.g. the Genius Bar), were fundamental in making Apple Stores both wildly popular among consumers, as well as one of the most profitable retailers on the planet, averaging $6000 in revenues per square foot (compared to $156 at JC Penney's, $194 at Kohl's and $171 at Macy's). So, not surprisingly, late in 2011 when Johnson decided to direct his Midas touch toward the ailing retail giant JC Penney, the retail world went giddy. Johnson's announcement as JC Penney's incoming CEO sent its stocks soaring 17.5% in a single day and Johnson himself was named the "2012 Newsmaker of the Year" by a leading retail publication.

A thorny retail problem had met its perfect foil: a transformational retail genius.

Fair and Square pricing strategy

Johnson's prescription for getting out of the vicious cycle that JC Penney was trapped in was to tackle all three problematic symptoms: the stodgy brand image, the poor in-store consumer experience and the deal-dependent pricing strategy. Soon after Johnson took over the helm at JC Penney, the brand logo was given a postmodern makeover. In place of the old logo, slick neon squares with a lowercase "jcp" in a simple and contemporary font were bandied around on their website, bricks-and-mortar stores and advertisements. Efforts were also under way to overhaul the in-store consumer experience by creating a "market square" shopping experience. The idea was to have discrete shops—including the likes of Martha Stewart, Izod, Arizona and Sephora—all laid out along pathways around a central square.

Another centerpiece of Johnson's strategy for JC Penney's revival was a total rebooting of its pricing strategy. He believed it was the critical piece that needed to be addressed in order to break out of the vicious cycle that

JC Penney had found itself trapped in. According to him, not only did the pricing strategy confuse consumers and promote an in-store mess that spoiled the consumer's experience, but it also fundamentally damaged the JC Penney brand. Referring to the hundreds of ever-present promotions, he remarked, "Every time we do that we're discounting the Penney's brand."

To remedy the situation Johnson unveiled the "Fair and Square" pricing strategy, which entailed three major changes. First, he replaced the labyrinthine system of deals and discounts with a simpler, more predictable three-tier pricing system: an "every day" price, a "monthly sale" price and a more deeply discounted "best" price. Note that while the structure was simplified, he made sure that the absolute level of discounts was *not* reduced. Second, he did away with the seemingly duplicitous "9"-ending sale prices. For example, instead of discounting a pair of sandals listed at $29.99 down to $14.99, he simply listed those sandals at an "every day" price of $15. Finally, heeding to the calls of the coupon-weary, Johnson got rid of the complicated system of coupons entirely.

These changes, Johnson reasoned, would offer a more appealing experience to consumers. To critics who pointed out that sales might suffer as a result of retracting the customary coupons and discounts, Johnson countered, "how do you explain the fact that people flock to Apple Stores to buy Apple products at full price when Wal-Mart, Best Buy, and Target carry most of them, often discounted in various ways, and Amazon carries them all—and doesn't charge sales tax! People come to the Apple Store for the experience—and they're willing to pay a premium for that." Thus at the heart of his reasoning was the firm belief that consumers like or dislike a store because of the experience that it has to offer. If you build a good consumer experience, they will come.

Approximately $1 billion was spent in 2012 alone to roll out the "Fair and Square" strategy in the form of engaging, humorous, high-profile TV ads that were aired during Oscars and other prominent time slots, and featured the popular comedienne Ellen DeGeneres.

The retail world waited in eager anticipation of the results. So what happened?

A wholly unexpected result

What ensued was a rocky roller-coaster ride that had many more downs than ups. It started well with the spectacular "Fair and Square" launch party in New York City for which Manhattan's Pier 57 was set abuzz with celebrities and über cool "jcp" installations. The television campaign featuring Ellen DeGeneres railing against duplicitous 9-ending prices and welcoming the simplicity of round prices (e.g. $14.99 versus $15.00), too, was hailed as "a breath of fresh air" and "sane." What followed this, however, was a completely different, and ominous, turn of events.

Even early on, the consumer response was tepid. When a reporter pointed this out, Johnson retorted, "What you can't do is chicken out," maintaining that good strategies fail because too often companies change course at the first sign of trouble. Materially, however, JC Penney was hurting: by the first three months of 2012 it had run losses of $163 million, same-store sales (for stores open more than one year) fell by 19%, the number of people visiting their stores dropped by 10%, and the number of people buying something at their stores, too, fell by 5%.

Johnson, however, did not chicken out and continued with the Fair and Square strategy. He acknowledged the problems in a 15 May interview to investors, "The transition has been tougher than we anticipated," but ultimately dismissed the poor response as part of the consumer education process, "We have got to get people to understand our pricing strategy." However, JC Penney's alarming free fall continued, and nine months down the line total sales dropped even further, down by 23.1% compared to the previous year, and the company racked up losses of $433 million. By the end of the fiscal year, sales fell even further, now down by 25%, and the losses stacked even higher, at $552 million. Not surprisingly, the stock market's notoriously fickle investors responded and JC Penney share prices fell by 51%.

It all culminated on 1 April 2013, when after a little over a year at the helm, Johnson was fired from JC Penney.

So what went wrong?

Lest this question is interpreted rhetorically, or interpreted as yet another example of recalcitrant leadership, we hasten to add that we think very highly of Ron Johnson. Johnson is a great marketing mind. In fact, each of the changes he introduced at JC Penney were identical to the ones he and his colleagues had introduced—with remarkable success—first at Target, then at Apple, and even at a Stanford University hospital. The combination of simplifying prices and improving the store experience firmly ensconced Target as a stylish brand in the consumer's mind, made Apple Stores a key driver of Apple's recent success, and put the patient back into focus at the Stanford hospital. So the question really is why, despite coming from a brilliant marketing mind and despite having been repeatedly successfully battle-tested at Target, Apple and Stanford, did these ideas fail?

Right on GO, wrong on STOP

We believe that at the core of JC Penney's troubles was the management's inability to correctly predict how their marketing actions would impact these GO and STOP signals and, as a consequence, the consumers' purchase decisions. It is an example of hedgehogian thinking and the side-effect neglect that we alluded to earlier.

It is an example of hedgehogian thinking and side-effect neglect

To better understand the nature of JC Penney's errors let's retrace our steps to Johnson's diagnosis of what ailed Penney. Johnson's vision for JC Penney was colored by his experience at Target and Apple stores. Do you recall our discussion on hedgehogian thinking in Chapter 1? This would be a good illustration of that. Johnson tried to replicate the formula that worked at Target and Apple stores, but without carefully considering and testing whether that formula would work at a mid-tier department store frequented by value-seeking consumers.

Johnson's diagnosis was twofold. First, Johnson believed that JC Penney did not elicit strong GO signals—the customer in-store experience was not as positive as he would have liked it to be. Johnson wanted to create a better store experience for JC Penney's shoppers; he firmly believed that if you build a good store experience, consumers will come and they will buy. The great success he achieved at Target and Apple by providing consumers with a compelling in-store experience had firmly ensconced this idea in his marketing DNA. Therefore, not surprisingly, he wanted to replicate the same success at JC Penney. Reflecting on the need for JC Penney to improve its consumer experience, Johnson had remarked that consumers essentially wanted "to belong to something deeper." To paraphrase his diagnosis in terms of the GO-STOP framework, Johnson believed that JC Penney was suffering from a weak GO signal, and that at the heart of this weak GO signal was the poor consumer experience.

Second, Johnson also believed that JC Penney's pricing strategy was confusing and untrustworthy, thus creating a STOP signal—negative feelings of mistrust and uncertainty. Johnson thought that the policy of incessant deals, discounts and sales was creating a STOP signal, inhibiting consumers from spending money at the store. Highlighting his concern about how these frequent promotions were keeping consumers away from JC Penney's stores, Johnson said: "It's like in junior high school, if you keep calling a girl and she doesn't call back, you seem desperate." In a presentation to [Penney's] investors in January 2012, Johnson went on to say that shoppers were not attracted to their stores and distrusted JC Penney because it offered so many discounts that it was impossible to know the real price. Johnson spoke to *Bloomberg Businessweek* and said: "I would like to build trust, and it starts with the price tag. I want truth in the price tag. I thought people were just tired of coupons." Thus, a second key component of his remedial action was the Fair and Square strategy aimed at weakening the STOP signal created by untrustworthy pricing. The Fair and Square pricing strategy involved ending frequent promotions, removing seemingly duplicitous 9-ending prices and discontinuing coupons.

In summary, Johnson's diagnosis was that: (a) poor store design and inferior product choices were weakening the GO signal, and (b) that the practice of frequent price promotions was strengthening the STOP signal. His prescription was, therefore, twofold: (a) improve the store design, and (b) take away the practice of frequent promotions.

His diagnosis, prescription and prediction were only partly correct. He was wise in discerning that the in-store experience is important. His recommendation on improving the in-store experience by redesigning the stores was also appropriate. This strategy would have definitely strengthened the GO signals for JC Penney consumers. But his assumption that frequent price promotions were strengthening the STOP signal and that doing away with frequent price promotions would weaken the STOP signal was unequivocally off the mark. In fact, taking away the familiar "sale signs" actually ended up significantly *strengthening* the STOP signal. Instead of making JC Penney merchandise more attractive, it made spending money at JC Penney more painful. Let's now examine this particular misstep in more detail.

JC Penney's management team assumed that excessive promotions created negative emotional responses—feelings of confusion, uncertainty and mistrust—in customers and thus inhibited purchase behavior. This premise is correct at a very abstract level—it is true that sometimes excessive deals, discounts and coupons can run the risk of damaging brand equity. In fact, in subsequent chapters we talk about several examples when a low price can hurt a brand by weakening the GO signal. But this happens only in specific situations. As we discuss in subsequent chapters in greater detail, this is more likely to happen when consumers use price as a signal of quality and consumers are in a quality-maximization or benefit-maximization mindset. Such price–quality inferences are more likely to manifest for expensive durables such as cars, fancy restaurants or medicinal products, not at discount stores.

However, this did not apply to JC Penney. Price promotions were not diluting the perceived quality of JC Penney's merchandise. The discounted prices were not making customers suspicious about the quality of the goods sold at JC Penney. Quite to the contrary, there was every reason to believe that price promotions had a positive effect on JC Penney customers—they were weakening the negative emotions associated with the pain of paying. For most regular JC Penney consumers, price promotion was weakening the STOP signal because it gave consumers a justification to buy—"It's on sale, so I would be saving by buying it." It reduced their pain of paying. In fact, stores like JC Penney have long conditioned their buyers to savor special deals, coupons and discounts. It was the price promotions and the "bargain hunt" feeling that these promotions fostered that attracted consumers to JC Penney stores. Mark Ellwood, the author of *Bargain Fever* (2013) captures this "bargain hunt" sentiment the best: "These are not women who feel taken advantage of by coupons and deals. To them, there's the thrill of the hunt – it's hunting and gathering with a credit card. No consumers have been complaining about discounts."

Evidence from other, similar competitor's experiments with abandoning coupons also pointed in the same direction. Consider the case of Macy's, JC Penney's archrival. After Macy's acquired May Co. in 2005, the number of discounts offered was drastically reduced. But sales fell, stock prices plummeted and Macy's managers soon abandoned the idea. At an April 2005 press conference, Karen Hoguet, Macy's chief financial officer (CFO), said: "People love these coupons. They love thinking they got us."

JC Penney could have learned from Macy's experience. It is quite evident that Penney's consumers would be of the same mindset. It is clear that the bulk of JC Penney's consumers loved clipping coupons and waiting for sales. Not surprisingly, JC Penney shoppers reacted adversely to the Fair and Square pricing strategy. On an NPR show an irate JC Penney shopper from Florida, Carol Vickery, expressed her frustration: "I come home and I cried over it, and my husband's looking at me, like, 'What's wrong?' I said, 'Penney's doesn't have sales anymore. I need my store back!'" The failed Fair and Square experiment is now part of Penney's checkered history. Soon after Johnson was ousted, a company spokesperson acknowledged: "While our prices continue to represent a tremendous value every day, we now understand that consumers are motivated by promotions and prefer to receive discounts through sales and coupons applied at the register."

In summary, the JC Penney debacle occurred mainly because managers had incorrect insights about the GO and STOP signals. They wrongly diagnosed that frequent price promotions caused uncertainty and confusion and strengthened the STOP signal. In reality, frequent price promotions served as a useful tool for weakening the STOP signal (at least for JC Penney's existing consumers). Naturally, then, their prediction as to what would happen when the Fair and Square antidote was administered, also went completely awry. In doing away with frequent price promotions, the managers inadvertently strengthened the STOP signal and significantly hurt sales. Thus, this is an example of the side-effect neglect that we spoke about earlier.

Isn't $19.99 the same as $20?

One of the elements of the Fair and Square pricing strategy was doing away with the age-old practice of 9-ending prices. In fact, as has already been mentioned, Johnson and his team made an expensive advertisement that showed Ellen DeGeneres making fun of the retailing practice of using 9-ending prices. These ads featured the comedienne in a store, lambasting a salesperson for the deceptive nature of the store's $14.99 prices (as opposed to the simplicity of $15) with her usual edgy sense of humor. We recommend readers to take a look at these hilarious ads (https://www.youtube.com/watch?v=K_78iVigjSI).

This ad did raise skepticism about the age-old retailing practice and made people wonder: do 9-ending prices and sale signs really matter that much? Do consumers perceive $19.99 to be that much lower than $20? Surely consumers see through such marketing gimmicks? We are willing to bet that if we asked consumers directly about the practice of 9-ending prices (versus rounded prices), most consumers would echo this skepticism. Reactions may vary, but it is very likely that a vast majority of consumers will simply make fun of such prices, and strongly deny that these promotional practices hold much sway over their shopping behaviors. At best, some might say that they are indifferent to them, if not totally dismissive of them. In fact, many of our friends chuckled and nodded in appreciation when the JC Penney Fair and Square campaign ads were aired on TV. They

reflect many consumers' naive or lay beliefs about the ineffectiveness of 9-ending prices.

However, results from several experiments—laboratory as well as field experiments—suggest that the skepticism is misplaced. Several carefully designed experiments have shown that 9-ending prices and sale signs have a strong impact on our shopping behaviors. It doesn't matter what consumers consciously say against their relative efficacy— these promotional effects are large and disproportionately so, widely prevalent across a diverse range of product categories and often exert their influence on the consumer in an *unconscious* manner. It is a robust effect: yet another instance where asking consumers is not as useful as testing through well-designed experiments.

Reading from left to right—the fast and frugal way

How do these 9-ending prices affect purchase decisions? Most robust psychological effects are multiply determined. That is, there are multiple psychological mechanisms that cause them. The 9-ending effect also operates through two distinct mechanisms. The first one is caused by left-digit anchoring in price comparisons. The left-digit anchoring effect is based on the notion that people read multi-digit numbers from left-to-right and, consequently, during price comparisons their magnitude judgments are anchored on the left-most digits. For example, the heuristic mind encodes the difference between $4.00 and $2.99 as "2 something" rather than as $1.01.

One of the co-authors of this book, Manoj Thomas (Cornell University), along with Vicki Morwitz (New York University), ran a series of laboratory experiments to study when 9-endings would influence perceptions of price magnitude. Their finding was quite straightforward: 9-endings influenced price perception when it resulted in a change in the left-most dollar digit (e.g. changing $3.00 to $2.99 changed the dollar digit), but 9-endings did not affect price perception when it did not change the left-most digit (e.g. changing $3.50 to $3.49 did not change the dollar digit). The left-digit anchoring effect can make a sale price look more attractive, if the consumer is comparing the regular price and the sale price. To get a first-hand experience of this heuristic in action, consider the following example: which of the two sale prices below—at Shop A or at Shop B— seem more attractive to you at first glance?

Shop A: regular price: $82.99   sale price: $50.00
Shop B: regular price: $82.98   sale price: $49.99

Retailers seem to be mindful of the left-digit effect in price comparisons; in fact, Robert Schindler of Rutgers University, who has done scores of studies on this effect, found that retailers are more likely to use 9-endings when the 9-ending will change the left-most dollar digit. Keith Coulter at

Clark University suggests that the left-digit effect may be enhanced when the cents are printed smaller, for example, 19^{99}.

This left-digit effect manifests not just in laboratory experiments, but also in real-world settings with non-trivial economic consequences. It has been shown that shoppers in grocery stores choose the product with lower dime digits without considering the cents digits. Buyers in the used car market pay disproportionately higher prices for cars whose mileage falls just below a 10,000-mile threshold. The left-digit effect even influences stock-market transactions. Traders are more likely to buy stocks priced one penny below whole dollar amounts.

Consumers might think that they are not fooled by the left-digit effect but many savvy retailers seem to be aware of the left-digit effect and use 9-ending prices to further increase value perceptions of their merchandise.

If only JC Penney managers had looked at this graph

There is yet another distinct psychological mechanism, probably a more pervasive one, through which 9-ending prices influence sales. And this one is very relevant to JC Penney. Independent of the left-digit effect (which manifests in comparative settings), 9-endings can serve as "sale signs" on their own and thus make the price seem more attractive than it is. A consumer is likely to infer that a product priced at $39.99 is more likely to be on sale than one priced at $38.00. Why might that be the case? Probably because they are used to seeing companies use 9-ending prices on products that are promoted. In the Pavlovian paradigm, one might say that consumers are conditioned to associate 9-endings with price promotions. If 9-endings make a price look more attractive, it then follows that removing 9-endings can make the price look less attractive and therefore make consumers less likely to make the purchase. This was conclusively demonstrated in a series of field experiments done by Eric Anderson and Duncan Simester, two marketing academics from Northwestern and MIT, respectively. One cannot but help wish that Ron Johnson or some other manager at JC Penney had seen the results of these studies (that were published in 2003) before they removed 9-endings and sale signs from the JC Penney stores.

Collaborating with national mail-order companies that sell moderately priced women's clothing, Anderson and Simester conducted elaborate field experiments that carefully tested the effect of removing 9-endings from prices. In one of the field experiments the authors worked with a mail-order company that has been regularly using 9-ending prices for the products listed in their catalog. Thus all their customers were accustomed to seeing 9-ending prices in the catalog. Note that this baseline scenario is very similar to what prevailed at JC Penney—JC Penney's customers were also accustomed to seeing 9-ending prices in the JC Penney stores. The researchers then created three versions of catalogs by changing the price-endings—a control version and two treatment versions. The control version had a 9-ending price (e.g. $39), which was the regular practice for this retailer. In the two treatment versions all prices were either increased by $1 or decreased by $1, so that price increases yielded price-endings of "0" (e.g. $40) and price decreases yielded price-endings of "8" (e.g. $38). The three versions of the catalogs were then distributed to separate, randomly chosen customer samples, with about 20,000 customers receiving each version. All of the customers had purchased from the catalog in the previous 18 months. Readers would note that this situation is quite representative of Ron Johnson's new pricing policy at JC Penney. By looking at the results of this study, Johnson and his team could have predicted the likely outcome at JC Penney if they were to abolish 9-endings. So what did Anderson and Simester find? They found that taking away 9-ending prices caused a drop in demand by around 26%. The researchers conducted a similar field study with another mail-order company whose extant policy was also to use 9-endings for the prices. The researchers created three versions of the catalogs—one with 9-ending prices (e.g. $39) and two treatment conditions where the price was either raised by $5 (e.g. $44) or lowered by $5 (e.g. $34). The results are summarized in Figure 3.1.

Again, taking away 9-ending prices caused a drop in demand by around 31%. A whopping 31%! This 26–31% drop in demand in the Anderson

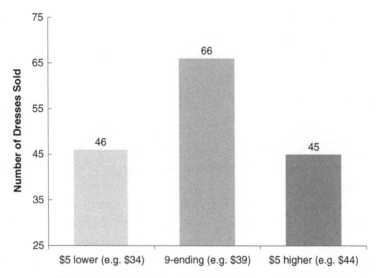

FIGURE 3.1 / The effect of price cues

Source: Data from Eric T. Anderson and Duncan Simester (2003), Effects of $9 Price Endings on Retail Sales: Evidence from Field Experiments, Quantitative Marketing and Economics, Vol. 1, No. 1, pp. 93–110; Eric T. Anderson and Duncan Simester (2003), Mind Your Pricing Cues, Harvard Business Review, Vol. 81, No. 9, pp. 96–103.

and Simester studies is uncannily similar to the sales decrease that JC Penney experienced when they implemented the Fair and Square pricing strategy (recall that JC Penney's sales fell by 25%). If only Ron Johnson had seen these results before changing the pricing policy at JC Penney.

Paying cash, emotionally

In order to understand why price cues have such an impact on purchase decisions, you have to first understand the role of emotions in payment decisions. Parting with money is painful and the proverbial "sale signs" (whether of the 9-ending or other types) alleviate this pain. Stated differently, prices elicit negative emotions and sale signs curb such emotions. In the GO-STOP parlance we can say that prices elicit STOP signals and sale signs can weaken such STOP signals.

Economists and others who subscribe to the rational homo economicus model of consumer behavior often question whether prices actually elicit emotional responses. Is the terminology "pain of payment" scientifically justified?

The answer is yes.

Recent studies have shown that processing price information activates the very same region of the brain that is associated with processing *physical* pain. One such study was conducted by an interdisciplinary dream team of academics from neuropsychology, marketing and behavioral economics comprising Brian Knutson (Stanford), Scott Rick (Carnegie), Elliott Wimmer (Stanford), Drazen Prelec (MIT) and George Loewenstein (Carnegie). Their study used functional magnetic resonance imaging, or functional MRI (fMRI), a brain-scanning technology, to study how the brain responds to various kinds of product-related stimuli.

As a brief methodological digression, note that the beauty of the fMRI method is that it does not rely on a shopper's conscious, self-report of whether he or she will buy or not buy. Self-reports, as we have said several times already, are noisy because consumers often do not know why they made a particular judgment or decision. In fMRI methods, it doesn't matter what the respondent consciously says; all the respondent has to do is look at the product, price or any other stimuli that he or she is exposed to, and then the patterns of brain activations are used by the researchers to *infer* and predict what the shopper will do. Many fMRI studies have shown that such patterns of brain activation (that the respondent is clearly not consciously aware of), compared to conscious self-reports, can more accurately predict a wide range of outcomes such as purchase decisions, product enjoyment, relative efficacy of different ads, political preferences and cessation activities (e.g. quitting smoking), to name a few.

Reverting back to the study in question, Knutson and his colleagues provided participants in their study with actual cash money and while participants' brains were being scanned by the fMRI machine they were exposed to a series of products that they could buy. Participants were free to not purchase any of the products shown in the study; they could walk away with the cash they were given. During the study participants went through a series of three critical exposures. First, they were shown the product without any price information. Second, they were shown the product along with the price information. Third, they were given the opportunity to purchase the product at the indicated price. At each stage, brain activation was recorded. Note that the three discrete steps allowed the researchers to isolate the effect of exposure to price from the effect of exposure to the product alone. They repeated this procedure for a wide range of products (approximately 80) across a wide range of prices (approximately $6–$60). The products included chocolates, gadgets (e.g. desk clip lamp, mood clock), appliances (e.g. smoothie maker, power toothbrush), books and DVDs. Outside of the scanner participants were also asked to self-report their attitudes toward the products and product categories that they had seen earlier. The main purpose of the study was to see: (a) which areas of the brain were activated when people saw the product alone versus when they saw the product in conjunction with price, and (b) whether the brain activation could accurately predict actual purchase behavior.

The results indicate that when participants were exposed to the product alone the nucleus accumbens was consistently activated. The nucleus accumbens is a region of the brain with dopamine receptors that are activated when we experience or anticipate something pleasant, such as making money or drinking something tasty. Even more relevant for purposes of our discussion, the study also showed that another region of the brain—the insula—was consistently activated when participants saw prices that they thought were excessive. The insula is a region of the brain that is activated when we smell something bad, see something disgusting or anticipate a painful shock. In fact, the greater the price differential (i.e. the difference between what participants were willing to pay and the displayed list price), the greater was the activation in the insula region. The very same pain centers of the brain that light up on experience (or anticipation) of physical pain, also lit up when the prices were too high.

More importantly, insula activation correctly predicted whether participants would buy or not buy an item: the greater the insula activation, the less likely that the item would be bought. Interestingly, insula activation predicted purchase behavior *independent* of the nucleus accumbens activation. In other words, insula activation correctly predicted whether participants would buy an item, even if participants happened to have been very excited about the product during the previous, product-only exposure stage (i.e. they earlier showed a high nucleus accumbens activation). In short, no matter how excited they were by the product, high price differentials acted as a STOP signal that inhibited the influence of the GO signal.

The finding from this study suggests that when Johnson took away the 9-ending prices, sale signs and coupons, effectively he might have increased the shopper's insula activation. In the typical JC Penney shopping environment prior to Johnson's changes, these sale signs reduced the subjective pain of payment that shoppers felt. In one stroke, the Fair and Square strategy might have increased that pain of payment by manifold.

The JC Penney saga illustrates one important point—price cues matter. Price cues matter because they reduce the pain of paying. Price cues matter because they weaken the STOP signals. Mindlessly removing price cues in a hedgehogian manner, and neglecting to anticipate the side effects of removing price cues on the STOP signal, can backfire.

4

Tata Nano, the world's cheapest car
Low price can backfire

If you have traveled to India, you might have been intrigued by a common sight on the country's streets—a family of four traveling on a two-wheeler. The father is usually on the driver's seat, carefully navigating the scooter through the chaotic traffic. The mother sits sidesaddle on the pillion seat, clutching on to her baby in her lap with one hand and holding on to the scooter with the other hand. The elder child, sandwiched between the father in the driver's seat and the mother on the pillion, wraps its arms around the father to avoid falling off the scooter.

It was this visual image that inspired Ratan Tata, the head of Tata Motors Limited—the second largest passenger vehicle manufacturer in India—to recognize a huge opportunity at the bottom of the pyramid. Cars are too expensive for an Indian middle-class family. For millions of people in India buying a car is a dream. Only the rich people can afford cars. Two wheelers—Vespa-type scooters, motorcycles and mopeds—are the dominant mode of personal transport in India. In 2009, 76% of all vehicle sales in India were two-wheelers. Tata figured that if his company could produce a car that appealed to the two-wheeler owners in India it would be a game changer.

This insight was the trigger for Tata Nano—the cheapest car in the world. When Ratan Tata conceived the idea of the people's car, he set a target price of $2000. How Tata arrived at that price point is not known to us, but at first blush the $2000 price point seems appropriate. Tata's main competitors in the Indian market were cars sold by Suzuki and Hyundai that were priced over $4000. So at $2000 the Nano was roughly half the cost of its nearest competitor. Moreover, since Tata's primary target market was two-wheeler owners, the price had to be comparable to the price of the popular two-wheelers—scooters and motorcycles that cost anywhere between $500 and $1500. So the $2000 price point was not only affordable for an upwardly mobile two-wheeler owner, but it was also much cheaper than other options available in the entry-level car market.

Tata's announcement to launch the Nano at $2000 created a sensation around the world. Launching the vehicle, Ratan Tata remarked: "I observed families riding on two-wheelers—the father driving the scooter, his young kid standing in front of him, his wife seated behind him holding a little baby. It led me to wonder whether one could conceive of a safe, affordable, all-weather form of transport for such a family. Tata Motors' engineers and designers gave their all for about four years to realize this goal. Today, we indeed have a People's Car." The media applauded Tata's visionary zeal and fondly labeled Nano as the "cheapest car in the world." Pundits predicted that the Nano will increase the penetration of cars not only in India but also in other developing countries. The tiny, egg-shaped car and its frugal engineering was a point of hot discussion at trade shows and engineering schools. A dismantled Nano was on exhibition at Cornell University's Herbert F. Johnson Museum of Art.

But when the car was finally launched in India, the consumer reception was tepid. Not many people wanted to buy a car that was labeled as the "cheapest car in the world." In December 2010, the *New York Times* ran a story on the Nano titled "Tata's Nano, the Car that Few Want to Buy."

What went wrong?

/ Too cheap, too cheap

From a pricing perspective, one reason for Tata Nano's initial failure was that it was perceived as too cheap. Yes, a product can be perceived to be too cheap.

A product can be perceived to be too cheap

Note the emphasis on *perception*, implying that it might have nothing to do with the actual price. It has more to do with consumers' subjective interpretation of price. We are not suggesting that the Nano should not have been priced at $2000. Instead, Tata Motors' misstep was *emphasizing the low price and communicating the low price* as the main reason to buy the Nano. It took a long time for the managers at Tata Motors to realize their communication gaffe—every time a reporter referred to the Nano as the "world's cheapest car" or the "low-cost car" or the "frugal car," the perceived quality of the car was taking a beating.

In Chapter 3 we described one type of pricing misstep—when managers' attempt to remove price cues unintentionally increased the strength of the STOP signal and thus inhibited consumers' from buying the product. In this chapter, we will describe another common pricing misstep—when managers attempt to weaken the STOP signal by lowering the price but it unintentionally ends up weakening the GO signal.

Price is an ambiguous cue that can be interpreted differently depending on the consumer's expectations and purchase mindset. A high price can cause pain of paying and thus trigger the STOP signal. This is more likely to happen when consumers are in a *pain-minimization mindset*. But sometimes a high price can do just the opposite—it can strengthen the GO signal. When consumers focus more on the functional, social and psychological benefits of the product, they are in a *benefit-maximization mindset*. Durables, medicines, luxury products and trips to fancy restaurants are often purchased in such a mindset. In such situations underpricing the product can, instead of weakening the STOP signal, actually weaken the GO signal. Stated differently, when quality is an important criterion, consumers evaluate products based on the adage

"you get what you pay for." In such cases, they are more sensitive to the GO signal than to the STOP signal. When the consumer's goal is to maximize quality or the benefits from a transaction, if the marketer focuses on minimizing the pain of paying by emphasizing low prices, then such a pricing strategy can backfire. That is what happened with Tata Nano.

A car is more than a bundle of functional benefits. Safety, fuel efficiency, price, comfort, space—all these are important considerations that influence a consumer's choice of a car. But there are other, arguably more important, factors that influence the purchase decision. The transition from a two-wheeler to a car is an important milestone for the burgeoning middle class in India. It signals a change in social status. When a family living in a middle-class neighborhood buys their first car, the friendly neighbors gather around it. The less friendly ones peer furtively through their windows. Some admire the new car. Others envy the owner's transition up the social ladder. The kids in the neighborhood clamor for a ride in the new car. It is also not uncommon for a priest to be brought in to "bless" the first car of the proud owner. Therefore, for this segment of car buyers, their purchase decision is as sensitive to the GO signal as it is to the STOP signal. Somewhat ironically, this is more likely for consumers in the lower-income group than those in the higher-income group. Of course, a consumer with low income would be constrained by a smaller budget, but within that small budget he or she seeks to maximize the social benefits of owning a car. The social signaling benefits of buying a car are more important for a poor, socially marginalized consumer than for a rich consumer who is higher up on the Maslovian hierarchy.

Nano did not offer this social signaling benefit.

The Nano, positioned as the cheapest car in the world, failed to provide the esteem and the social status that a typical first-car purchase provided in India. In terms of social signaling, buying a Nano was not very different from buying a two-wheeler. One cannot hope to move up the social ladder by acquiring a car that has become famous as the poor person's car. Thus, in our GO-STOP signal parlance, the unrelenting emphasis on the lower price of Nano backfired because it weakened the GO signal and thus reduced purchase intentions.

In fact, a few years after the launch, in an interview with CNBC, Ratan Tata himself acknowledged that tagging Tata Nano as "the cheapest car" might have hurt its prospects: "It became termed as a cheapest car by the public and, I am sorry to say, by ourselves, not by me, but the company when it was marketing it. I think that is unfortunate."

Targeting the right consumer

The thing about brand positioning is that it is sticky. Once consumers have a particular image of a brand, it cannot be changed easily. As is often said—the first impression lasts for a long time. Tata Motors could not change the "cheapest car" image for the Nano, at least not in the short term. How the marketers advertise the car, or how engineers or consumer reports rate the car is not nearly as consequential as how consumers talk about the car. No matter what marketing actions they take to reposition themselves, the Nano is likely to be stuck with the "cheapest car" image for the next few years. No amount of advertising and image management can undo this damage overnight.

Therefore, the managers at the Tata Motor Company, quite wisely, decided to change the target market for the Nano. If folks around you do not like your image and you cannot change your image overnight, what do you do? One easy solution is to hang out with people who will like your image. In like vein, instead of attempting to sell the car to consumers who consider their car's brand as a signal of their social status, managers at Tata Motors found a segment of consumers who were looking for a small, no-frills, inexpensive car—the richer Indians who were looking for a second car. The Nano was an ideal choice for the rich father who was looking to buy an inexpensive entry-level car for his college-going daughter. Or for the husband who wanted to gift a car to his wife so that she does not have to take the luxury family sedan for her shopping trips. For these families, since they already had a luxury sedan, the second car was not a signal of social identity. They just wanted something that did not cost much and was easy to maintain. Their dominant criterion was pain-minimization, and the Tata Nano was priced to minimize their pain of paying. In other words, the richer Indian families looking for a second car were more sensitive to the STOP signal than to the GO signal. Thus the car aimed at the bottom of the pyramid found (some) salvation, ironically, at the top of the pyramid.

The company also decided to shift their focus to markets where Nano was not stigmatized by the "cheapest car" tag: "Maybe it [Nano] gets launched in another country like Indonesia, where it doesn't have the stigma and the new image comes back to India. Or maybe as a changed product that gets marketed in Europe. There's a lot of interest in Nano outside India," Tata said in an interview on CNBC.

The lesson from the Tata Nano case study is that sometimes trying to weaken the STOP signal by lowering price can misfire; low prices can also inadvertently weaken the GO signal. It is a classic case of side-effect neglect caused by hedgehogian thinking. The management team at Tata failed to anticipate the adverse side effects of their proposed marketing action on the GO signal.

It's not just income

There is another lesson to be learned from the Tata Nano example. The Nano example highlights an important but often misunderstood aspect of GO and STOP signal sensitivity. It is tempting to assume that sensitivity to GO and STOP signals are determined only by demographic variables such as income and wealth. When we present the concepts of GO-sensitivity and STOP-sensitivity to MBA students and seasoned executives, it is not unusual to find an enthusiastic participant exclaiming: "Ah, I get it! The rich folks are more sensitive to the GO signal, and the poor folks are more sensitive to the STOP signal." Students like to simplify assumptions when it comes to predicting consumer behavior. They like to group consumers into neatly divided segments based on observable variables such as income and wealth. Such simple segmentation strategies make the prediction problem seem more tractable. Lamentably, predicting consumer behavior is not that simple.

The Nano case study clearly shows that income is not a reliable predictor of GO- and STOP-signal sensitivity. In this case, somewhat ironically, it was the higher-income people who were more inclined to buy a no-frills inexpensive second car. Since they had already satisfied their social signaling need by purchasing a luxury sedan as their first car, they were less concerned about its social signaling value or perceived quality while evaluating the second car. In contrast, the lower-income people, who were upgrading from two-wheelers to cars, were more focused on maximizing the social identity value from the purchase. Therefore, they were more perturbed by the adverse social signaling of the low price. They were also more concerned about buying a low quality car that might increase their service and repair cost. Therefore, ironically the low price of Tata Nano was an inhibitory factor for the low-income segment, but less so for the high-income segment. So, although income and wealth levels can influence benefit-maximization or pain-minimization mindsets, it is important to remember that these mindsets are not uniquely determined by income and wealth.

The placebo effect of price

Does a lower price really reduce the perceived quality of the product? Can such biases in perception influence actual behavior?

The Tata Nano case study suggests that they do. In fact, if you flip through any book on pricing you will come across several other case studies that make the same point. But social scientists do not accept case studies as sufficient evidence for the postulated causal mechanisms. For conclusive evidence they turn to controlled experiments. A series of such controlled experiments on price–quality effects were run by three brilliant scholars—Baba Shiv, Ziv Carmon and Dan Ariely, professors of marketing at Stanford, INSEAD and Duke business schools, respectively.

These researchers recruited 125 college students to participate in a study. Their task was to solve a series of word-jumble puzzles. For example, when presented with a string of letters TUPPIL, the participants were expected to unscramble it to form the word PULPIT. They were given 30 minutes and asked to solve as many puzzles as they could. Before they started solving the puzzles, the experimenters asked them to drink SoBe Adrenaline Rush—an energy drink that many college students consume to increase their mental acuity. Most of the participants were familiar with this energy drink. Even if they had not consumed the drink previously, most of them were aware that SoBe is a performance-enhancing drink. In fact, even if you are completely unfamiliar with this brand, if you take one look at its packaging you will figure out that the drink is designed to boost your energy. The descriptor of SoBe Adrenaline Rush—High Performance Energy Supplement—is boldly printed on the bottle. Given this messaging, the experimenters hypothesized that drinking SoBe would increase participants' expectations about their ability to solve puzzles—and that this expectation would, in turn, motivate them to actually solve more puzzles. This is the well-known placebo effect. Although placebo effects are typically discussed in the context of pills and medical interventions, such effects can be caused also by marketing actions. Consumers who believe that a product will enhance their performance might actually perform better simply because they expect better performance from themselves. Anyone who has given or received an inspiring pep talk knows what we are talking about—people's expectations can influence their actual performance. Expectations also play a critical role in consumers' price–quality inferences. We discuss the role of expectations in greater detail in Chapter 6.

Here comes the critical manipulation in the experiment.

Participants had to pay for the energy drink and unbeknown to them the amount they paid varied across conditions. Half the participants were told they would be charged $1.89—the regular price of SoBe at retail outlets. The other half were told that they had to pay only $0.89 because the researchers had bought SoBe at a discount as a part of an institutional purchase. The experimenters were interested in testing whether this subtle manipulation of price would influence the number of puzzles the participants would solve. They reasoned that if the participants considered price as a signal of quality, then those who bought SoBe at a discounted price should be suspicious (albeit not consciously) of the efficacy of the drink. And this suspicion should weaken the placebo effect of the drink. That is, consumers who got the product at discounted price should solve fewer puzzles than those who got the drink at the regular price. This was indeed the case; participants who purchased SoBe at the discounted price solved fewer puzzles relative to those who purchased the exact same drink at a higher price. Those who consumed the lower-priced drink solved 7.7 puzzles in the given 30 minutes while those who consumed the higher-priced drink solved 9.5 puzzles. Price, in this case, had a placebo effect on performance.

The SoBe study conceptually replicates the finding in the Tata Nano case study. Consumers may not like products that are too cheap. This price–quality effect manifests for cars, electronic goods, restaurant food and even grocery products. The critical difference between the Tata Nano case study and the SoBe study is that the latter was a controlled laboratory experiment. Since the Tata Nano case study did not have a control group, we cannot uniquely identify the effects of price. In contrast, everything in the SoBe experiment was controlled; the drink was the same, the word puzzle was the same, and researchers used random assignment to control for individual differences in participants' intelligence, ability to solve puzzles, etc. The only factor that was changed was the price. Half the participants paid the regular price for the drink, whereas half paid a lower, discounted price for the same drink. Thus, based on these results we can confidently claim that a lower price can hurt the perceived quality of a product.

5

When not to discount

Inexpensive wines and employee discount for everyone

You get what you pay for

Popular Folk Wisdom

In Chapter 4 we discussed the case of Tata Nano. Ratan Tata, the visionary head of Tata Motor Company in India, observed families riding on two-wheelers—the father driving the scooter, his young child standing in front of him, his wife seated behind him holding a baby—and resolved to build a safe and affordable car for such a low-income Indian family. His target was to launch a people's car priced at $2000. His engineers and designers worked tirelessly for four years and realized this goal. Tata Nano, the low-income people's car, was launched. But the low-income people balked at purchasing the inexpensive car. Instead they preferred to buy a used Maruti Suzuki or Hyundai car from the second-hand car market at around the same price, because Nano's low price reduced the attractiveness of the cars. The Tata Nano case study and the SoBe experiment described in Chapter 4 suggest that people often rely on the popular folk wisdom "you get what you pay for." They view low-priced products with suspicion, and instead of increasing sales, low prices can reduce sales. In this chapter, we further explore this intriguing psychological phenomenon.

General Motors' employee discounts

What would you do if customers seem unenthusiastic about the brands and models of automobiles that you manufacture and are reluctant to purchase them?

This is the grim situation that greeted Mark LaNeve, General Motors' (GM) top North American marketing and sales executive, when he took over the helm at GM in 2005. The signs were ominous. Sales at GM had fallen by 7% compared to the previous year. GM's overall market share in North America had slipped to 25.1% from the previous year's 29%. It now took 91 days to clear its inventory from the dealers' lots as compared to 45 days for its Japanese rivals, and the average age of the buyers even for some of its popular brands simply did not paint a rosy future (e.g. average age of Buick buyers was 63 years). The company's top marketing executives huddled into a conference room to brainstorm. Should GM try to improve the models they were launching, or lower the prices, or offer better incentives such as deeper rebates and discounts, advertise differently, or encourage their dealers and salespeople to do a better job? All sorts of ideas were considered but nothing seemed to pop out in terms of a panacea.

The breakthrough idea came from a GM veteran, Steve Hill, who was the brand and retail director at GM. Hill had always been fascinated by the power of the employee discount program that he as an employee of GM had access to. As part of the employee discount program each GM employee could not only avail of a special discount for themselves but also provide the same discount to one friend, family member or colleague. He had always observed that the best way for him to get someone to buy a car was to whip out his GM employee ID card and give them that discount. It was a powerful hook for prospective buyers when they were told that they could avail the same "inside" rate as the rest of the "GM family" does. Hill had successfully used this simple tactic to introduce many a friend to GM products. His winning idea was quite simple: why not offer the same discount to everyone and call it the "Employee Discount for Everyone" scheme? Everyone in the conference room jumped at the idea.

It took the CEO Rick Wagoner and CFO John Devine less than ten minutes to sign off on this idea, and it took around just 20 days (5–26 May) for GM to complete fashioning out the creatives, issuing casting calls, shooting the ads and training dealers on how to implement the discount scheme. The program ran for three months (June–August 2005) and was acclaimed as a great success as it drove up demand by 16% in those months.

Imitation is the best form of flattery; soon all Detroit automakers followed suit with similar schemes of their own. The press was replete with articles celebrating GM's simple stroke of genius, the Employee Discount for Everyone scheme.

However, in the months that followed immediately after the scheme expired in August 2005, the Employee Discount for Everyone scheme turned out to be as pyrrhic as any victory can ever get. It is true that demand did go up as much as 16% during those three months when the scheme was running, but it turns out that the sales bump was simply borrowing from the future. In other words, people were simply buying ahead of when they normally would have bought. By October 2005 GM's sales were down by 25.9%, which not only wiped out the earlier 16% gain, but it also created a hole that the company could not dig itself out of. In January 2006, acknowledging that the scheme did not address the problem it was intended to address, in an interview to the *Wall Street Journal* online, Mark LaNeve said: "Hindsight being 20/20, I probably wouldn't have done it."

What went wrong?

In our opinion, this was another case of a misdiagnosis caused by hedgehogian thinking. The management team failed to address the root cause of what ailed GM's cars. The management reasoned that providing the employee discount would significantly weaken the STOP signal for their cars. And yes, they were right in the short term: the attractive incentives did indeed lead to a temporary uptake in demand of about 16%. But the underlying problem with GM cars is not that they elicited a strong STOP signal in prospective customers' minds; rather, the problem is that GM cars, like those from other Detroit automakers, do not energize and attract the customers. In essence, GM cars elicited very weak GO signals. Naturally, then, making changes to the STOP signal (via lower prices) will not have any lasting benefits if the root problem lies with the GO signal.

It is no divination that the root problem for GM's cars was in the GO signal and not in the STOP signal. Albeit not couched in the GO-STOP signal terminology, this fact can be deduced from countless auto industry reports and articles by McKinsey and Co., the Economist Intelligence Unit (EIU), *Business Week* and *Forbes*, to name a few. In driving tests conducted by third parties such as Consumer Reports or *Car and Driver* magazine, GM's cars usually fared worse than their Japanese counterparts. For example, prior to 2008, it would not be unusual for even Chevy Malibu (one of GM's bestselling models) to finish dead last in its segment in the *Car and Driver* magazine's comparison test. Even if you refused to consider what is under the hood and wanted to ignore driving tests conducted by the "experts" at Consumer Reports and *Car and Driver* magazine, it's not as if GM's design and styling points were superlative. These cars looked more boxy and less sleek than their Japanese competitors did. Besides falling behind on actual performance and style-and-look points, GM's auto brands were also not supported by the kind of perception-enhancing, brand-building advertising that the Japanese auto brands were supported with. Instead of conveying brand benefits, a bulk (approximately 55%) of the "big three's" marketing budget went into rebates and incentives. Thus, it is quite apparent that the GO signal associated with GM's cars was weak; there was nothing about GM's cars that stuck out to the customer and attracted potential buyers toward them.

Second, a cursory look at the prevalent prices would reveal that GM's cars were not priced high compared to other automakers (e.g. Japanese automakers). If anything, the contrary was true: GM's cars were, effectively, already lower priced. The average discount on a GM car was $7200 compared to the industry average of $5000 and an average of $3130 for the Japanese automakers. So it could not have been strong price-induced STOP signals that were holding back prospective customers from buying GM cars.

In summary, when Mark LaNeve took over GM, the nature of the problem of "poor sales" that he inherited was different from what he perceived it to be. The problem was not that GM's cars were otherwise wonderful and it was only a high price that was triggering the STOP signal and leading to poor sales. Rather, the problem was that *despite* having lower prices compared to that of its competitors (e.g. GM's $7200 discounts versus Japanese competitors' $3130 discounts), GM's auto sales were still suffering. The problem clearly was in the GO signal, not in the STOP signal. Thus, a revival strategy centered on providing more discounts that would further weaken the STOP signal is tantamount to a wrong diagnosis leading to a wrong prescription. In short, for GM it was a classic case of hedgehogian thinking that led managers to squander their resources on marketing tactics based on incorrect consumer insights.

Are consumers lying about the placebo effect of price?

Hilke Plassmann, a marketing professor at INSEAD, and her co-authors conducted an interesting experiment to examine the price placebo effects on the brain. Their study used functional magnetic resonance imaging, or functional MRI (fMRI), to study patterns of activations in the brain caused by price placebo. As discussed in Chapter 4, fMRI is an imaging procedure that measures brain activity by detecting associated changes in blood flow. Brain activity or neuronal activation, as scientists like to call it, is linked with cerebral blood flow. When an area of the brain is in use, blood flow to that region also increases. So, by monitoring blood flow to a particular part of the brain, scientists can monitor the extent to which that part is activated by the stimulus. Plassmann and her fellow researchers relied on this principle to investigate the placebo effect at the brain level.

They scanned the brains of 20 unsuspecting participants in an experiment while they tasted different wines. The ostensible purpose of the experiment was to study the effect of degustation time on perceived flavors. The participants were told they would be sampling five different Cabernet Sauvignons. They tasted each wine several times in a random order. To avoid spillover effects, there was a rinse period between each trial. They were also informed about the price of the wine. The prices ranged from

$5 to $90. The participants' task was to rate the pleasantness of each wine. The fMRI machine scanned their brains while they engaged in the tasting task. The researchers examined how the pleasantness ratings and the brain activations changed for each wine.

Although the participants in this study were told that they would taste five different wines, actually this was not the case. Two of the wines were used twice; once it was presented as a low-priced wine and once as a high-priced wine. Specifically, one of the Cabernet Sauvignons was presented half of the time at $90 and half of the time at $10. Another wine was presented half of the time at $5 and half of the time at $45. The researchers found that, as predicted, price did influence the taste of the wines. Participants reported the exact same wine as better tasting when it was priced higher.

However, a skeptic could question the veracity of participants' reports. Most psychologists worth their salt would not accept participants' self-reports at their face value. It is not unusual for participants to lie, consciously or unconsciously. Here is where the fMRI reports come in handy. Brain scan reports do not lie. The researchers in this study examined the brain scan reports to test whether the participants were merely reporting that the expensive wine tasted better or if it actually (i.e. physiologically) tasted better. Their exami-nation revealed that increasing the price of a wine increased the activation in an area of the brain called the medial orbitofrontal cortex. A lot of past research has shown that this area of the brain gets activated when we process a reward. The medial orbitofrontal cortex is engaged when people receive a reward or avoid a negative outcome. So the fact that higher prices increased the activations in the medial orbito-frontal cortex suggests that participants were not lying; they actually *experienced* more expensive wines to be more pleasant in taste.

In summary, the lesson from the Tata Nano and GM case studies and the SoBe and wine-pricing experiments is that marketers should not empha-size low prices when it can weaken the GO signal. This is all the more important when consumers' purchase decisions are relatively more sensi-tive to changes in the GO signal.

6

chapter

Avoid discordant pricing

Do you know your consumer's mindset?

> What's good for the goose isn't necessarily good for the gander.
>
> Old English saying

Let's take an example of two restaurateurs in New York City. One owns Café Cubano and the other owns the Fountains restaurant and bar. The restaurateurs are considering dropping their menu prices in the hope that lower prices will attract more customers. But they are concerned whether lowering the menu price will hurt the perceived quality of the food. Can menu price affect the perceived quality of food? Will lowering the price hurt food quality ratings at these restaurants?

When will lower price hurt a brand and when will it help a brand? This is a question that many thoughtful marketers have grappled with at one time or another.

It is common knowledge that lower prices can increase market shares for many brands. However, we also know that marketers should not emphasize lower prices when it can weaken the GO signal because in such cases lower prices can backfire and reduce market shares. We have discussed several such case studies in the previous chapters—how getting labeled as the cheapest car stalled Tata Nano's sales, how steep discounts exacerbated the decline of General Motors' reputation and how low wine prices make the wine actually taste unappealing. But we have not yet discussed when a low price will weaken the GO signal and when it will not.

A tale of two restaurants

The two restaurants—Café Cubano and the Fountains—operate in two different market segments. Café Cubano is a casual dining Cuban/Caribbean restaurant on the upper west side of Manhattan. The Fountains restaurant and bar is a formal fine dining property located in Brooklyn Heights near the Brooklyn Bridge.

The Cuban/Caribbean restaurant has a relaxed format with an extensive menu and a substantial takeout business. It features, according to its advertisements, "one of the best Café Cubanos north of Miami along with traditional Cuban homestyle cooking." Specialties include "savory mofongo, plentiful paella, ropa vieja, oxtail stew and more." The well-lit, brightly colored décor and Latin music create an ambience that is conducive to conversation, as customers take their seats at Formica-clad tables and enjoy a variety of tropical shakes or modestly priced wines. Customer reviews exhibit considerable inconsistency, from raves to rants, with many falling between those extremes. Business is good enough to turn a profit, and Café Cubano is known among New Yorkers as a venue that delivers good Cuban food at an economical price. The average price of a dinner is $19.

The Fountains is an upscale, formal dining place across the Brooklyn Bridge from Manhattan, a location that has become increasingly popular. The room is portrayed in its ads as a place with "rustic elegance" with one reviewer remarking on its "sophisticated and quiet setting." It finds itself on a list of restaurants with "romantic settings," with another reviewer noting that it has a distinctive New York City character. It features Brooklyn artifacts in its décor and intimate, polished-wood bar. The Fountains serves American and some continental-inspired cuisine and local ethnic dishes.

It advertises a specially prepared hanger steak as its "signature dish." The average price of a dinner is $36.

Will lowering the menu price have the same effect on both these restaurants? Or will it hurt more at the Café Cubano than at the Fountains?

Casual versus formal restaurants

To study whether price-perceived quality relation varies for casual and formal restaurants one of the co-authors of this book, Manoj Thomas (Cornell University), along with Vicki Morwitz (New York University) and Leonard Lodish (Wharton School), examined the relationship between menu price and customers' food ratings. They analyzed data from the 2002 Zagat restaurant survey of New York City restaurants (the Zagat company collects customers' ratings of restaurants in several cities around the world). The researchers selected the Zagat ratings for New York City as it has a large number of restaurants of various cuisines and styles. This popular restaurant guide lists customers' ratings of food along with the price of an average meal (including one drink and tip) for several hundred eateries in the city. Additionally, the Zagat guide also lists the ratings of décor and service. Ratings for food quality, décor and service ranged from zero (poor) to 30 (perfection).

The restaurant evaluations used in the Zagat guide came from over 29,000 respondents, and 1,564 restaurants in New York City.

Thomas, Morwitz and Lodish examined the price-perceived quality relationship separately in two clusters of restaurants. Each of the 1564 restaurants was assigned to one of the two clusters based on consumers' ratings of décor and service. These two clusters were formed using a statistical procedure called cluster analysis. The restaurants were clustered only on the basis of décor and service ratings, without any prior assumption on how the two groups differ in their food ratings or price levels. The researchers used the clustering analysis to assign restaurants with lower décor and service ratings to the casual restaurants cluster, while those with higher décor and service ratings were assigned to the formal restaurants cluster. Then, within each cluster, they examined the relation between menu price and food ratings. Each of the two clusters had more than 700 restaurants, which reassures us that the results reported here are likely to be robust.

So what did these researchers find?

The top panel in Figure 6.1 depicts the relationship between menu price and food ratings for restaurants that were categorized as formal restaurants. In the cluster of formal restaurants, where restaurants had relatively high décor and service ratings, price was a significant predictor of perceived food quality. The higher the menu price, the better the food ratings. Conversely, formal restaurants with lower menu prices were associated with lower food ratings.

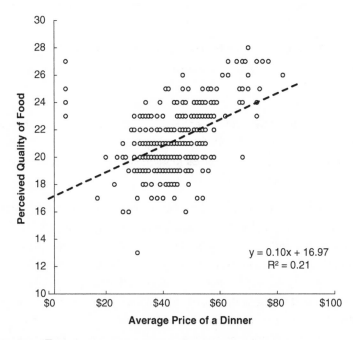

FIGURE 6.1 / Menu price and food ratings for formal restaurants

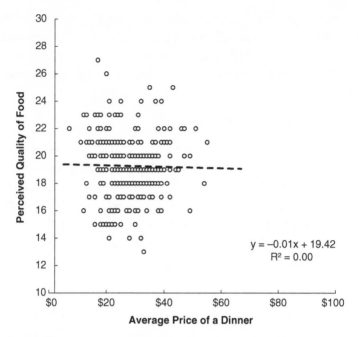

FIGURE 6.2 / **Menu price and food ratings for casual restaurants**

Source: Data from Zagat Survey (2002), Zagat 2002 Survey for New York City Restaurants, New York: Zagat Survey, LLC.

However, in the other cluster—the cluster of casual restaurants—price was not at all correlated with food rating. Figure 6.2 depicts the relation between menu price and perceived food quality for casual restaurants. The correlation was close to zero.

The owners of Café Cubano and the Fountains restaurant and bar can gain some useful insights from the scatter plots and regression results shown in Figures 6.1 and 6.2. The results suggest that if the menu price at the Fountains is lower than expected, then it will hurt the restaurant's food ratings. In fact, our regression model suggests that for every dollar drop in price, the food rating at the Fountains will drop by .13 units on the Zagat scale. Dropping the menu price by $7.70 would reduce the food rating by almost one full point on the Zagat scale. Such a drop in the perceived quality of food could dilute the restaurant's positioning. Some of its core customers might no longer consider it a formal dining place and might take their patronage elsewhere. So reducing the menu price seems like a double-edged sword for the Fountains.

However, for casual restaurants there is no association between menu price and food rating. This suggests that reducing the menu price will not affect Café Cubano's Zagat food rating. Since price discounts will not dilute the positioning of Café Cubano, it might be a viable strategy for this restaurant. That is, Café Cubano can drop its menu price and claim that it is offering "the same taste at a lower price." But such a claim from the Fountains might not be considered credible; it might backfire.

What is good for the goose is not necessarily good for the gander.

Top-down processing

Why does price influence food ratings of formal restaurants but not influence ratings of casual restaurants? The short answer to the complex question is top-down processing. Our mind works in a top-down fashion. Top-down processing often enables us to make smart deductive inferences. But sometimes it can distort our expectations in irrational and inexplicable ways.

The following popular example, often used in cognitive psychology textbooks, succinctly illustrates how top-down processing influences subjective interpretations. Consider the two words below:

THE CAT

Source: http://en.wikipedia.org/wiki/Context_effect

When presented with the above two words, most people "see" the words THE CAT despite the unusual middle letters in these two words. In the first word, they interpret the middle letter as H while they interpret the *same* middle letter as A in the second word. Take a closer look and you will notice that the middle letters in both words are identical. Yet, they are interpreted differently. This happens because the activation of the knowledge of English words and spelling patterns causes the brain to subjectively perceive the middle letter in the context of the word in which it is embedded.[1] More generally, top-down processing effects refer to the influence of schematic knowledge and contextual information on perception and cognition.

Top-down processing exerts a powerful influence on our everyday judgments. It can influence the manner in which we interpret people's

---

[1] We ascribe causal agency to the brain or the mind to portray that some of these processes might be occurring unconsciously in the brain without the person's awareness or volition.

behaviors and traits in order to make social judgments, and the manner in which we evaluate product features and price to make purchase decisions.

Solomon Asch, an American social psychologist, conducted a series of experiments to study how we form impressions of other people. His experiments illustrated how our knowledge and expectations influence the interpretation of new information. In one of his experiments, Asch asked one group of participants to form impressions about a person described to have the following attributes:

envious, stubborn, critical, impulsive, industrious, intelligent

A second group of participants were given the same list of attributes with one seemingly trivial difference. The order of presentation of the attributes was reversed:

intelligent, industrious, impulsive, critical, stubborn, envious

Even though the list of attributes was identical, the second group formed more favorable impressions of the person described by these attributes. The second group perceived the target as an able person with some shortcomings, whereas the first group perceived the target as a problematic person. More importantly, the subjective meanings of ambivalent attributes such as *impulsive* changed across the two groups; the first group interpreted ambivalent attributes negatively whereas the second group interpreted them positively.

Price cognition and social cognition are influenced by the same cognitive procedures. Just as top-down processing can influence social judgments, top-down processing can also influence consumers' interpretation of price. When a restaurant has good décor and professional service, a higher menu price is interpreted as a signal of better quality. Consider a restaurant with the following three attributes:

good décor, professional service, high price

Now, consider another restaurant with the following attributes:

casual décor, quick service, high price

The first restaurant resembles our mental image of the prototypical formal restaurant. And this resemblance seduces the brain to interpret higher menu price as a signal of better quality. In contrast, even though the price information is the same at the second restaurant, it does not resemble our mental prototype of a formal restaurant. So in such cases, higher menu prices are not interpreted as signals of food quality.

Causation and correlation

At this point, we can imagine some discerning readers sitting up and saying "Hold your horses, correlation does not imply causation!" They might ask: how can we be sure from the Zagat study that menu price can affect food ratings? Isn't it likely that restaurants with higher food ratings charge more whereas those with lower food ratings charge less?

Well, it is a plausible alternative account for the observed pattern of data. But this alternative account seems unlikely because if that were the case, then we should have seen a similar pattern for casual restaurants as well. Casual restaurants with higher food ratings should have charged more money than those with lower food ratings. But that was not the case, as you can see in Figure 6.2.

Nevertheless, the fact remains that the results from the Zagat study are correlational and, therefore, cannot be completely trusted unless we verify it by running an experiment. We have said this before, we say this again here, and we will keep repeating this: experiments are the best and perhaps the only way to identify cause-and-effect relationships.

So Thomas, Morwitz and Lodish conducted a follow-up study. They ran a laboratory experiment to study whether merely changing menu prices can influence consumers' expectations about food quality at a restaurant, and whether this effect of changing menu prices would vary across casual and formal restaurants. Such an experiment is the only way to test causality; it would confirm that it is the change in menu price that is affecting perceived quality of food, rather than the other way around.

The experiment had one more purpose. The researchers went beyond price–quality inferences and examined the effect of price on participants' behavioral intentions—whether they will dine at the restaurant. After all, marketers care more about consumers' behaviors than their inferences. The researchers hypothesized that the effect of price on consumers' behavioral intentions will depend not only on the type of restaurant, but it will also depend on the mindset of the consumer. If quality is not a relevant dimension in a consumption context, and consumers are not trying to maximize quality, then price–quality inferences would not affect consumer behavior.

Date dinner and casual dinner

Not just factors that influence a priori *expectations* of food quality but even factors that influence *relevance* of quality can affect a consumer's response to price. For a higher price to increase purchase intentions, not only should consumers interpret the higher price as a signal of superior quality, but they also should seek and cherish superior quality. That is, they should be in a benefit-maximization mindset rather than in a pain-minimization mindset.

Based on this logic, Thomas, Morwitz and Lodish hypothesized that the effect of menu price on GO signals will depend not only on the type of restaurant, but also on the consumption occasion. That is, higher menu prices will improve ratings of food at formal restaurants but not for casual restaurants; additionally, this effect is more likely to influence behavior when people are more sensitive to ratings of food—such as when they are on a date. Price–quality inferences are less likely to influence consumer behavior when they are seeking a quick and convenient restaurant, such as for a casual weekday lunch.

The researchers designed their experiment to test whether menu prices are evaluated differently under different circumstances. They recruited around 200 students studying at New York University and asked them to evaluate a new restaurant called Hudson's Bounty. The participants in this restaurant were given two bits of information—a restaurant review and a menu. However, unbeknown to the participants, the experimenters created two different versions of the reviews and menus. In one version Hudson's Bounty was described as a casual restaurant (casual restaurant condition) whereas in the other review it was described as a formal restaurant (formal restaurant condition). Half the participants saw one version, while the other half saw the other version.

Similarly, there were two versions of menus. In the high price condition, the prices of the food items were in the range of $8.00 to $29.00 (high price condition). In the low price condition, the prices of food items were in the range of $3.25 to $11.50 (low price condition). The descriptions of the food items and all other details remained identical in all the conditions, only the prices changed and the types of restaurants.

Participants were randomly sorted into four groups and were assigned to one of the four experimental conditions created by crossing the restaurant type and menu price: casual–high priced, casual–low priced, formal–high priced, formal–low priced.

After reading the menu and the review, participants were asked a series of question. They were asked to indicate how likely they were to "have dinner with a special date at Hudson's Bounty." This was a situation when participants were expected to be more sensitive to food rating. They were also asked to indicate how likely they were to "have a casual dinner with friends at Hudson's Bounty." In this situation, participants were expected to be relatively *less* sensitive to food rating. Participants indicated their responses to both these questions on seven-point scales where higher scores indicated a higher likelihood of dining at Hudson's Bounty.

First let us consider the special dinner with a date. Figure 6.3 depicts how restaurant type and menu price interactively influenced dining intentions for a special dinner with a date.

When the restaurant was being considered for a special date, for the formal restaurant a higher menu price increased participants' intentions to dine at that restaurant. That is, the more expensive the formal restaurant, the more likely were participants to go there for a date. This result is consistent with what we observed in Figure 6.1 (i.e. the Zagat

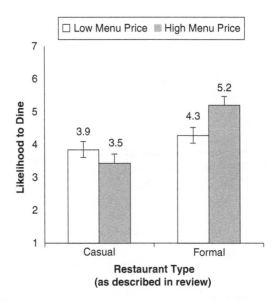

FIGURE 6.3 / Dinner with a date

data for the formal restaurants cluster; higher menu prices are associated with better food ratings at formal restaurants). But when the restaurant was described as a casual restaurant, a higher menu price did not increase the intention to go there on a date. Again, this result is consistent with what we observed in Figure 6.2 (i.e. the Zagat data for casual restaurants cluster; menu price does not affect food ratings at casual restaurants).

Interestingly, the effect of price on purchase intentions completely reversed when the participants considered the restaurant for a casual dinner with friends. As depicted in Figure 6.4, a higher menu price *reduced* purchase intentions irrespective of the type of restaurant. When the participants considered the restaurant for a casual dinner with friends, they presumably valued economy and convenience more than the gastronomic experience and social signaling value of the restaurant. So they did not care about price–quality inferences, even for formal restaurants. When participants did not care much about quality, the higher menu price, instead of making the restaurant look more appealing, strengthened the pain of payment and thus reduced purchase intentions.

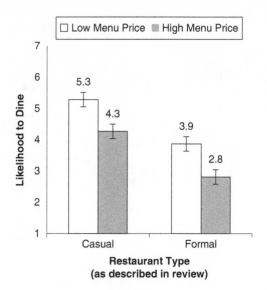

FIGURE 6.4 ⁄ **Casual dinner with friends**

Source: Data from Manoj Thomas, Vicki Morwitz and Leonard Lodish (2009), When Does Expensive Food Taste Better? Top-Down and Bottom-Up Processing in Price-Quality Inferences, Cornell University Working Paper.

As shown in Figure 6.4, for a casual dinner with friends, the higher menu price, instead of strengthening the GO signal, strengthened the STOP signal. These results tell us that for higher prices to strengthen the GO signal two different conditions should be met. First, the higher price should be interpreted as a signal of better quality. Second, consumers should be in a benefit-maximization mindset rather than in a pain-minimization mindset; that is, they should care more about superior quality than about reducing the pain of payment.

⁄ Discordant pricing

Now let us revert to the question that marked the beginning of this chapter: When will a lower price weaken the GO signal and when will it not? The lesson from the Tata Nano and GM case studies and the SoBe and wine-pricing experiments is that low prices can weaken the GO signal. Furthermore, in this chapter we saw that it is not always the case. Sometimes a lower price can be discordant with the consumer's mindset, and sometimes a higher price can be discordant with the consumer's mindset. So the key is in understanding when a particular pricing strategy will be discordant with the consumer mindset. Let us try to answer this question through inductive generalization; we will first consider the pattern of consumer behavior across a few examples, and then try to inductively infer the general principle of discordant pricing.

The restaurant studies described earlier in this chapter suggest that if a restaurant with good décor and excellent service uses a lower-priced menu it can be considered discordant by prospective customers who are looking for a special dinner. This discordance will weaken the GO signal, particularly if the prospective consumer is seeking the extra benefits associated with the higher price. In contrast, when people are seeking a restaurant for a casual meal—one that is convenient and not too expensive—the restaurant with a lower-priced menu will seem more appealing relative than those with higher-priced menus. So when consumers are looking for a casual meal, higher menu prices might be considered as discordant. This discordance will strengthen the STOP signal.

As an example, people are willing to spend $4 for a cup of coffee at Starbucks, but they expect a similar cup of coffee to cost $1 at McDonald's. If Starbucks were to drop its price to $1, then its price would be seen as being discordant with its brand image and over time it will weaken the brand's GO signal potency among its loyal customers. Conversely, if McDonald's were to increase its price to $4, then its price would be seen as being discordant with customers' expectations of good value and it will strengthen the STOP signal among value-seeking customers.

Here is another example. People are willing to pay $50,000 for a BMW sedan, but they expect a Hyundai to cost around $20,000. If BMW were to drop its price to $20,000, then BMW aficionados will see the price as being discordant with their mental image of the brand and the marquee will lose its sheen among its core base. This will weaken the GO signals for BMW fans. Conversely, if Hyundai were to increase its price to $50,000, then its price would be seen as being discordant with customers' expectations and the price will trigger a STOP signal among prospective buyers.

Now let us try to inductively infer the generalizable psychological principle of pricing discordance that underlies all these examples.

These examples illustrate that discordance between customers' mindset and marketers' pricing strategy can hurt the sales of a brand. If customers are in a *pain-minimization mindset* and are trying to minimize their spending, then their purchase intentions will be more sensitive to changes in STOP signal than to changes in GO signal. In such a situation, trying to strengthen the GO signal by using higher prices can be discordant.

Conversely, if consumers care about the functional, social or psychological benefits of the product and are willing to pay more for the benefits they seek, then they will expect the price to be higher than that of mediocre quality products. When consumers are in *benefit-maximization mindset*, their purchase intention will be more sensitive to changes in the GO signal than to changes in STOP signal—because product benefits are cues that trigger the GO signal. In such a situation, trying to weaken the STOP signal by using lower prices can be discordant. The discordant pricing principle can be summarized as follows:

1) If a brand's price is discordant with consumers' mindset, then it will reduce their willingness to buy the brand.
2) When purchase intentions are more sensitive to functional, social or psychological benefits of the product (benefit-maximization mindset), lower prices can be seen as discordant and can reduce sales.
3) When purchase intentions are more sensitive to the pain of paying (pain-minimization mindset), higher prices can be seen as discordant and can reduce sales.

The discordant pricing principle is schematically depicted in Figure 6.5. The X-axis of this 2 x 2 schematic reflects the marketer mindset and the Y-axis

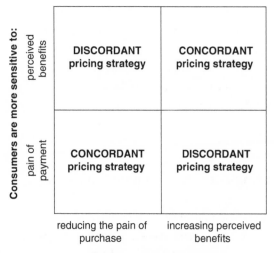

Consumers are more sensitive to:

	reducing the pain of purchase	increasing perceived benefits
perceived benefits	DISCORDANT pricing strategy	CONCORDANT pricing strategy
pain of payment	CONCORDANT pricing strategy	DISCORDANT pricing strategy

Pricing strategy focuses on:

FIGURE 6.5 / Concordant and discordant pricing strategy

reflects the consumer mindset. When the two are aligned, it leads to concordant pricing. When the two are incongruent, it results in discordant pricing.

The notion of discordance is pivoted on consumers' purchase mindset. A purchase mindset is a cognitive orientation—the assumptions, beliefs and preferences that guide a consumer's marketplace judgments and purchase decisions. In the benefit-maximization mindset, consumers are more sensitive to cues that trigger GO signals such as product quality, prestige and special features. In the pain-minimization mindset, consumers are more sensitive to cues that trigger the STOP signal such as the pain of parting with money, unfairness and risk. Discordance between consumers' purchase mindset and the pricing strategy can lead to pricing mistakes.

Discordance is pivoted on consumers' purchase mindset

What factors influence consumers' purchase mindset? When are consumers more sensitive to cues that trigger the GO signal and when are they more sensitive to cues that trigger the STOP signal?

Purchase mindsets are influenced by the interplay of several
factors. However, three main factors deserve some
discussion: (a) marketing cues, (b) social factors
and (c) segment traits. Figure 6.6 presents a
schematic representation of how the factors
interactively influence consumers' purchase
mindsets.

Marketing cues and purchase mindsets

Consumers' purchase mindsets can be primed by marketing communication and product cues.[2] Brand name is an important marketing cue. Some
brand names can put consumers in a benefit-maximization mindset, which
in turn can make them interpret a high price as a signal of more benefits.
Other brands name can put consumers in a pain-minimization purchase
mindset, which in turn makes them evaluate a higher price unfavorably.
Akshay Rao (University of Minnesota) and Kent Monroe (University of
Illinois at Urbana-Champaign) have concluded, based on a meta-analysis
of scores of research papers on price–quality effects, that these effects
depend on brand names and store names. They concluded that while some
product and store brands increase price–quality effects, other product and
store brands reduce price–quality effects.

Brand names and store names change the effect of price on quality
because they can prime different goals. In an interesting experiment, social
psychologist Tanya Chartrand (Duke University) along with consumer psychologists Joel Huber (Duke University), Baba Shiv (Stanford University)
and Robin Tanner (University of Wisconsin-Madison) tested whether
brand names can prime thrift and prestige goals. These researchers used
subliminal priming technique wherein participants were presented with

---

[2] Cues in the shopping environment can change expectations as well as mindsets. Cues
can make consumers more likely to interpret price as a signal of quality and at the same
time product cues can also make their purchase decisions more sensitive to perceived
quality.

brand names outside their foveal visual field but within their parafoveal visual field. Half the participants were exposed to prestigious brand names—Tiffany, Neiman Marcus and Nordstrom. The other half were exposed to thrifty brands—Walmart, K-Mart and Dollar Store. After this priming task, all participants were asked to respond to an ostensibly unrelated task. They had to choose between the following two brands of socks:

Option A: Nike socks at $5.25 per pair

Option B: Hanes socks at $6.00 for two pairs

The first option offers more prestige but it is also more expensive. The second option is less prestigious but offers more bang for the buck—two pairs of Hanes socks for the price of one pair of Nike socks. The researchers found that participants who were primed with high-end retail store brand names were more likely to choose the expensive Nike socks. In our GO-STOP parlance, priming people with high-end store brand names put them in a benefit-maximization mindset and thus increased their relative sensitivity to benefit-related cues that trigger the GO signal. They cared more about prestige and product quality than about economy. In contrast, priming people with low-end retail store brand names put them in a pain-minimization mindset and made them more sensitive to pain-related cues that trigger the STOP signal. They did not care much about prestige; they were more concerned about curbing wasteful spending, which made the Hanes socks look more appealing to them.

Not only brand names and store names but other marketing cues such as packaging, logo, advertising and promotional tactics can influence consumers' purchase mindsets. So how consumers evaluate prices depends quite a bit on the marketing cues that the companies use.

Social factors and purchase mindsets

Consumers' purchase mindsets can also be affected by factors that are outside of marketers' control. For instance, social pressure can influence consumers' purchase mindsets. Even mere social presence, that is, the mere presence of others around us, can change our purchase behaviors. Jennifer Argo (University of Alberta), Darren Dahl (University of British Columbia) and Rajesh Manchanda (University of Manitoba) conducted a brilliant experiment to test the effect of mere social presence on consumers' purchase mindsets. These researchers hypothesized that the mere presence of other people will motivate consumers to engage in impression management behaviors. This can increase their propensity to buy more expensive and premium brands and avoid cheap store brands. Volunteers who showed up to participate in their experiment were given $5 and were asked to go to the university store and purchase a package of four AA batteries. They could buy any brand available in the store and the purchased product as well as the remaining money was theirs to keep.

Without informing the unsuspecting participants, the researchers manipulated the presence versus absence of other shoppers around them while they were shopping. Some participants were randomly assigned to the shopping-with-social-presence condition, whereas others were assigned to the shopping-without-social-presence condition. When participants randomly assigned to the shopping-with-social-presence condition went to the battery display aisle, they saw either one or three other shoppers standing two feet away from them. The remaining participants (who were assigned to shopping-without-social-presence condition) shopped without having any other shoppers nearby. The researchers found that mere social presence changed participants' shopping behavior in an interesting manner. When no other shopper was present nearby, only 33% of the participants purchased the most expensive batteries in the store (Duracell/Energizer at $4.29). When one other shopper was present near the battery display aisle, 42% of the participants purchased the most expensive batteries. When three other shoppers were present nearby, 63% of the participants purchased the most expensive batteries. The mere presence of three shoppers almost doubled participants' propensity to buy the most expensive brand!

In terms of our GO-STOP model, mere social presence can activate the desire to be viewed in a positive light, the desire to be liked and respected. These desires can put people in a benefit-maximization mindset and

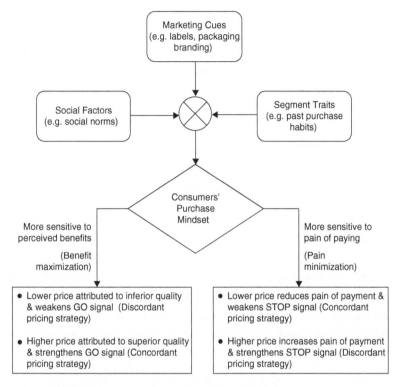

FIGURE 6.6 / Factors that influence consumers' mindset

thus increase their sensitivity to benefit-related cues that can trigger GO signals. This, in turn, can make them interpret the price of a product as a signal of social status rather than as a measure of economic sacrifice.

Segment traits and purchase mindsets

Finally, segment characteristics could also influence consumers' purchase mindset. Who is more likely to be in benefit-maximization mindset— someone who has a Bottega Veneta bag, silk-and-lace Eres undergarments and a Jaeger-LeCoultre watch or someone who buys bags and undergarments that are on promotion at Macy's and JC Penney's? Past behaviors are reliable indicators of future behavior. So if a consumer's past purchases suggest an innate or chronic tendency to be in a benefit-maximization mindset, the chances are that his or her future purchases will be influenced by a similar tendency. It would be reasonable to conclude that this consumer has some innate characteristics that make him or her more likely to be in a benefit-maximization mindset rather than in a pain-minimization mindset. So marketers often use past purchases to segment consumers into benefit-maximization and pain-minimization mindsets.

Know your consumers' expectations and mindsets

In summary, a higher price is a double-edged sword. Sometimes higher prices can trigger the STOP signal and reduce sales. However, at other times higher prices can strengthen GO signals and increase sales. The results from several case studies and experiments help us to identify when a higher price will strengthen GO signals. For higher prices to strengthen GO signals, two conditions must be met: the higher price must be interpreted as a signal of better quality, and consumers must care more about better quality than about reducing their pain of paying.

Higher prices are likely to be interpreted as signals of better quality when other cues—brand name, packaging, design, décor, service—create an expectation of superior quality. Based on these cues when consumers expect the product to be of superior quality, their mind subjectively interprets the price as a signal of superior quality. However, it is not just consumers' expectations, their mindsets also influence the promotional effect of higher price on purchase decisions. If the core users of the brand are in a benefit-maximization mindset, then setting a high price might be more concordant with the mindset. However, if the core users are in a pain-minimization mindset, then higher prices would be discordant with the mindset. So two important determinants of a brand's pricing strategy are the target consumers' expectations and mindset—whether the target consumer expects the product to be of superior quality and whether he or she is likely to be in a benefit-maximization mindset or a pain-minimization mindset.

chapter 7

Paying for medicines and Tickle Me Elmo

Beware of unfairness cues

> Unfairness is in the eye of the beholder.
>
> Anonymous

Victoria's (not so) secret prices

On 4 January 1996 a young woman named Denise Katzman filed a class action lawsuit against Victoria's Secret, the popular lingerie brand. Her bone of contention? A colleague of hers received a catalog in which the same product was offered at a lower price. Was there a lot of money at stake? Not really. She was offered the product at a $10 discount while her colleague was offered a $25 discount. The absurdity of the situation becomes a little more apparent if you take into account the legal fees—$5000—she had to pay for the entire litigation process. It gets even curioser and curioser! It turns out that her colleague who was unfairly "favored" by Victoria's Secret was male, which likely (though not definitively) indicates that her colleague may not even be in a position to "enjoy" that differential discount.

Consumer reactions to prices can be very varied. On the one hand consumers seem to rail against the unfairness of minor price differences, but on the other hand many consumers seem quite comfortable with the idea of price variations and complex pricing schemes.

Consumers understand the utopian reality of "one-price-for-all"

Consumers are not naive about how firms operate and conduct their business; they fully understand that the ideal of "one-price-for-all" is largely a myth. Consumers routinely witness price variations: lower price for matinee tickets for theater shows; higher prices for dinners at 7pm (versus 5pm); discounted movie tickets for seniors, military personnel, children and students; higher prices for baseball games during the play-off (versus regular) season; price-matching policies at grocery stores; airline ticket prices varying over time—sometimes even varying in a matter of a few days or hours; lower prices for loyal customers; lower prices for coupon holders; relatively low but wildly varying prices at auction sites such as Piceline.com; and, indeed, despite regulatory furor against the car service Uber in certain parts of the world, consumers have accorded a very warm welcome to this service whose prices could vary from minute to minute.

Consumers seem to understand the utopian reality of "one-price-for-all." They accept, and sometimes even zealously embrace—like in Uber's case—the idea that the same item could be both priced differently to different people and priced differently at different times.

Or do they?

While consumers agree with the idea of price variations at an abstract level, their actual reactions tell a very different story. Newspapers are replete with cases of consumer backlash when prices change or differ. Many seem to be irrational overreactions, such as the Victoria's Secret incident described above. These sorts of occurrences are numerous and are hard to explain using the rational utility-maximizing model of consumer behavior. Consider below some additional such incidents, which show that consumers can react very strongly to price changes/ differences.

If you thought that the $15 difference between the two Victoria's Secret coupons is a substantial monetary amount, note that many of these cases of protest emerge even when very low price-differentials are at stake.

Amazon's $3.50 furor

Sometime in 2000 Amazon experimented with its prices online. In particular, one group of customers was charged a lower price, compared to another group of customers, for the same DVD title. This led to a howl of vehement protests from consumers, which careened into a media and public relations disaster for Amazon. The price difference, though, was not very large by any stretch of the imagination: one group was charged $22.74 and the other group was charged $26.94 for the same DVD. A mere $3.50 difference!

For many of these cases, what is surprising is that consumers might agree to a certain kind of pricing scheme, in principle, but then balk when it comes to specific instances. The next two incidents highlight this kind of inconsistency.

If you get more of a good, shouldn't you pay more?

Most consumers readily agree that if you get more of a good, you should pay more. Thus, consumers will readily accept (and expect) the large-size versions of a product (e.g. a cup of Starbucks coffee, a box of Tide detergent) to be priced higher than their medium and small counterparts. The logic is simple and straightforward: the large-size versions contain more of the raw materials and therefore cost more to manufacture; therefore, they should be priced higher to the consumer. By the same logic, larger sizes of clothing (e.g. XL, XXL or Plus sizes) should be priced higher than smaller ones (e.g. petite or small sizes) because considerably higher amounts of cloth go into producing the larger sizes. In fact, for most brands of clothing (e.g. Gap, Old Navy, Banana Republic), the manufacturers who produce the clothing for them charge these brands a 15% premium for manufacturing the Plus sizes. It therefore makes perfect sense for these brands to charge their end customers a 15% premium for the larger sizes. If it costs more to make, it should be priced higher. Following this logic one popular catalog company (name withheld due to confidentiality reasons) decided to charge a relatively modest 10% premium for its larger Plus sizes. The results were damning—there was a 28% drop in demand! For obvious reasons the company immediately discontinued this pricing scheme.

Surely playoff tickets should be more expensive than regular season tickets?

Another pricing scheme that consumers readily agree to is that ticket prices for certain critical games (e.g. Major League Baseball playoff games, or World Cup Soccer knockout games) should be higher than those of less critical games (e.g. MLB regular season games or World Cup Soccer league stage games). Here too, the logic is clear: the quality of a game is likely to be higher during the "knockout" stages of a tournament, when a lot more is at stake, than during the "regular" stages of the tournament. Therefore, it makes sense that the "deeper" you go into a season, the more you pay for game tickets. Fans understand this logic and readily agree to it, which is why despite an average ticket price of $3480 the Super Bowl 2014 was completely sold out many months before the event.

The NBA Eastern Conference Semifinals in 1997, however, was a totally different story.

New York Knicks versus Miami Heat

Once upon a time, long ago (c.1990s), the New York Knicks used to be really good and featured regularly in the basketball playoffs! In 1997, the New York Knicks and the Miami Heat met at the Eastern Conference Semifinals. The two battled it out in a classic best-of-seven series games. For the first four games the tickets were priced at $20, $30 and $40, depending on the quality of the seats. These four games ended up being completely sold out. Obviously, ticket prices were not yet declared for the remaining games since a team could sweep the series 4–0 in the very first four games, obviating the need for the last three games. However, a clean sweep did not happen and Game 5 had to be scheduled. Game 5 had the fans on tenterhooks. For the Knicks fans it could be the series-winning game (the Knicks were leading 3–1); for the Heat fans, it could be the now-or-never game that finally turns the tide in their favor (and there was plenty of hope as the game was to be played on home court, in Miami). This was the fourth year in a row that the two teams had met during the playoffs, and the tension was palpable. It promised to be a truly exciting and high-quality game. Naturally, then, in keeping with the criticality of the game, the organizers now increased the ticket prices of the potentially series-deciding (or series-turning, depending on which fans' perspective you look at) Game 5 to $50, $80 and $90, respectively.

Almost immediately, pandemonium ensued. Fans protested against these prices and there was widespread public outrage. In fact, fan indignation was so strong that many fans boycotted Game 5 and it ended up being one of the few playoff games in NBA history that wasn't sold out. Moreover, fans continued to protest and the organizers were compelled to lower the prices for Game 7, the series-deciding game, back to $20, $30 and $40! Thus, as this case shows, albeit fans agree with the idea in principle, they don't always want to pay more for better games.

The reader might think that this kind of outrage occurs because the incidents recounted so far—lingerie, DVD/movies, clothing, basketball games—are about products and services that we hold very dear to our hearts (e.g. the US is reputed to be a sports-crazy nation). But, surprisingly, this expression of outrage occurs even for categories that are not so important to us.

Tickle Me Elmo, but the prices aren't funny

An outrage about the rising prices of essentials such as gasoline or staple foods is understandable. Sometimes situational circumstances make an item an "essential"—like how a snow shovel becomes an essential after a snowstorm. Thus, not surprisingly, US consumers were outraged when gasoline prices crossed the $4 per gallon mark, when 99-cent surgical masks started selling for $10 during the SARS scare and when flashlights were sold at enormous premiums after a power outage in 2003. Consumers say that their outrage is justified because these items are essentials; they would not have reacted strongly if the item was not essential.

But in reality consumers regularly rail against price increases for non-essentials too. Take the case of Tickle Me Elmo, which, arguably, is a non-essential for most of us. Yet virulent consumer protests against the high prices of Tickle Me Elmo (and, more recently, other versions of this adorable doll) have become an annual affair. And these are not just empty threats that allow consumers to vent their frustration. In fact, in 1996 the protests became so vehement that the power of legislation was mobilized against Fisher-Price, the makers of Tickle Me Elmo.

For those pointing to the inexorable tug of heartstrings when a child cries, the feelings of guilt, or the inflexible demands of children throwing a "hissy fit," the authors would like to point out that we don't always give in to our children's every demand, nor do we always attempt to mobilize legislation. Parents could always walk away from Elmo. Yet there is something special about this incident that goes beyond the usual explanations of logic and emotion, something that we will come back to later in this chapter. However, for now it will suffice to say that we would be hard pressed to explain the exceptionally strong reactions to Tickle Me Elmo's prices, purely on rational and logical grounds.

Consider, for example, the scenes outside a Toys "R" Us store in suburban Virginia, where a press conference was called by consumers and their political representatives on 23 November 2006. Participants in this press conference were dozens of members of Congress, including Republican Senator John McCain from Arizona, the then Speaker of the House; Democrat Nancy Pelosi; and the House Commerce Committee Chairman, John Dingell. These legislative heavyweights were surrounded by a mob of angry parents and sobbing children. Against this backdrop, John Dingell let loose the first salvo, announcing that he would ask the Federal Trade Commission to investigate illegal price fixing by Fisher-Price: "Parents are demanding congressional action. We have strong evidence that Fisher-Price has intentionally constricted the supply in order to create an illegal shortage, and that retailers are engaging in price gouging activity." Joining in this melee Nancy Pelosi remarked: "Thanks to the quest for profits of America's toy manufacturers, this won't be a Merry Christmas for hundreds of thousands of needy children this year—including some of my own grandkids. When will corporate America understand that greed isn't a family value?" Holding up an Elmo doll with a $99 price tag, she further remarked: "If this is not price gouging, what is?"

I am sure that readers can guess what happened next—the press conference was interrupted by unruly parents who tried to snatch the doll away from Speaker Pelosi!

Why do some price increases (or differences)—such as the Victoria's Secret, Amazon, clothing catalog, Knicks-Heat and Elmo examples—lead to incendiary customer reactions? And why do other similar price increases—such as the theater, movie, grocery store and baseball examples we mentioned at the beginning of the chapter—barely eke out a whimper of protest?

"Unfair" prices activate the STOP signal

At the heart of these incendiary consumer reactions is the notion of "unfairness" of the price increase or price difference. Unfairness, like beauty, is in the eye of the beholder. Further, these feelings of "unfairness" are not based on rational calculations of utility. Rather, the role of heuristic inferences looms large. Consumers use fast and frugal heuristics to make inferences about whether it *feels* "unfair" for a firm to charge a particular price. The emphasis is on whether a particular price *feels* unfair subjectively, not whether it is objectively justified. Therefore, an understanding of the drivers of "unfairness" is critical as these feelings of "unfairness" amplify the STOP signal and turn the consumer away from the product. Not only that, a feeling of "unfairness" can even drive the consumer to punish the firm for its alleged "unfairness."

Price increases and price differences are inevitable. Sometimes these price changes are a function of necessity (e.g. at times of inflation when raw material costs increase), and sometimes these changes are a function of technology enabled arbitrage opportunities (e.g. sophisticated algorithms in online stores that vary price depending on the user's profile and willingness to pay). These price increases run the risk of activating and amplifying the STOP signal. Interestingly, however, not all price increases affect the STOP signal equally. As the examples discussed illustrate, some are accepted reasonably well, while some end up inciting public outrage, negative word-of-mouth campaigns, active exhortations to boycott the firm, efforts to politically legislate the firm's actions, and pursuit of other punitive actions. Common to all the incidents that spark outrage and activate the STOP signal are consumers' feelings of "unfairness" regarding the price change or price difference.

So when will a price increase or a price difference be deemed "unfair"? What triggers and drives these feelings of "unfairness"? Are there certain factors that exacerbate or attenuate the feeling of "unfairness"? If so, what can managers and public policy makers do to avoid or shield their organizations from it?

When will a price (change) be deemed "unfair" and strengthen the STOP signal?

At the outset it is important to note that most consumers do not actively evaluate the "unfairness" of a price. The average consumer is not a vigilante who is actively trolling supermarket aisles and hunting around for the slightest whiff of an "unfair" price (and the offending firm) to pick a bone with. Most consumers are too preoccupied with their personal, professional and social lives to be active arbitrators of the unfairness of prices. Thus, the notion of "unfairness" of prices usually lays dormant in the consumer's mind.

A checklist for determining whether a price change will spark protests of "unfairness" and strengthen the STOP signal is provided in Figure 7.1.

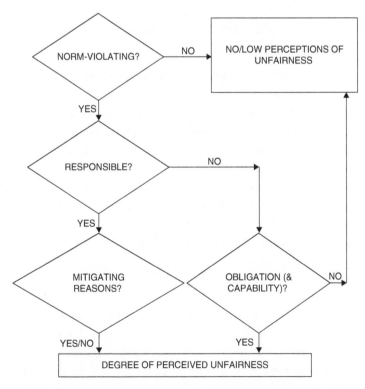

FIGURE 7.1 When will a price increase (or price difference) be deemed "unfair" and strengthen the STOP signal?

To correctly predict the extent to which judgments of "unfairness" will run rampant, like it did in the examples described earlier, managers and policy makers need to ask themselves four critical questions:

- Q1) Is the price increase (or price difference) likely to be perceived as *norm-violating*?
- Q2) Is the firm likely to be perceived as *responsible* for the norm-violating price increase (or price difference)?
- Q3) What is the perceived *reason* for the norm-violating price increase (or price difference)? Is it likely to mitigate perceptions of unfairness?
- Q4) Is the firm perceived to have an *obligation* (and *capability*) to prevent the norm-violating price increase (or price difference)?

Let's discuss each of these in more detail.

Q1: Is the price increase (or price difference) likely to be perceived as norm-violating?

In the chain of reasoning that leads to perceptions of an "unfair" price, the first link relates to whether or not a price increase (or a price difference) is perceived to violate a norm. This is the very first question that managers need to ask themselves—is the price change that is being contemplated, whether it is a price increase for all customers or a price difference across different segments of customers, likely to be perceived as norm-violating? If the answer to this question is no, then perceptions of price "unfairness" are unlikely. However, if the answer to this question is in the affirmative, then perceptions of price "unfairness" are likely to arise, and managers should be on their guard for such a possibility.

So when is a price increase (or price difference) likely to be perceived as "norm-violating" in nature?

There are two broad ways in which a price increase (or a price difference) can be perceived by consumers to be norm-violating: (a) when it violates norms of usual (business) practice, and (b) when it violates a moral norm. Let's look at some cases studies that illustrate such norm-violations.

Violations of usual-practice norms

Price increases and price differences, no matter how justifiable from a rational economic perspective, will run into trouble when they violate established business practices that customers are accustomed to.

For example, in recent years airlines have had to deal with a steep increase in the price of aviation fuel. The increase in fuel cost has been passed on to consumers, partly, via *direct increases* in the price of airline tickets. In part, some of the increase has been passed on to consumers *indirectly*, by charging for checked-in luggage and for snacks, meals and drinks during the flight. Here is another way to recoup the increased fuel cost—charge for checked-in luggage according to how far the person (and therefore the luggage) is travelling. This is a logical economic rationale. After all, transporting a piece of luggage from New York to Sydney consumes more fuel than transporting the same luggage from New York to Paris. So why not start charging for checked-in luggage in proportion to the distance that it will travel?

Violations of usual-practice norms?? But it makes perfect economic sense!

While the rationale for this kind of distance-based luggage pricing is economically sound (and just), it is almost surely likely to lead to howls of protest. This is because consumers are simply not used to being charged for their checked-in luggage in such a fashion—it simply violates what they are used to. If consumers are not used to it, they will not feel comfortable with the price increase, and declare the price change "unfair." In fact, this is one of the reasons why charging for checked-in luggage has begun with baby-steps, starting with a flat fee for the second bag. Many airlines have already started charging for any checked-in luggage, not just the second bag onward. Some industry observers anticipate that, ultimately, checked-in luggage will be charged based on the distance it travels. However, as of now, this practice is likely to face strong headwinds because it is a departure from business-as-usual.

The large-size clothing example we discussed earlier also fits here. Recall that large-size clothing, typically, costs 15% more to manufacture; therefore, charging a slight premium for large-size clothing makes good economic sense and is easily justifiable. However, when a firm started charging 10% higher prices for its large-size clothing, consumer demand for the large sizes fell by a whopping 28%. In fact, the researchers involved in that study, Duncan Simester (MIT) and Eric Anderson (Northwestern), were able to clearly isolate that at least 20% of that 28% decline in demand was due to consumer misgivings about an "unfair" price. Even though the price premium is based on an economically sound rationale, consumers are used to seeing different sizes of clothing priced very similarly. As already mentioned, they are used to such pricing schemes for other product categories such as coffee and detergents, where larger sizes are priced higher. However, for the category of clothing that is simply not an established practice—consumers are just not accustomed to it. As a result, consumers thought the price increase to be "unfair." Thus, anytime a price increase or price difference deviates from business-as-usual, managers have reasons to worry even if that increase or difference is backed by sound logic.

Violations of moral norms

Let's now look at a different source of norm-violations that might lead to indictments of "unfair" prices. These norm-violations have less to do with deviations from usual business practices that consumers have grown accustomed to; rather, these violations have more to do with deviations from moral norms. Certain price increases and price differences simply feel morally wrong to consumers and can inflate perceptions of unfairness.

Given that morality is subjective, varying drastically across cultures and even across individuals within a nation culture, is it at all possible for managers to anticipate whether a price increase or price difference will violate a moral norm?

Recent research evidence shows that there are some common "foundations" of morality that consistently appear across cultures and individuals. The pioneering work of Jonathan Haidt of New York University suggests that there are six "moral foundations" that drive many moral judgments. While Haidt and his collaborators did not study moral judgments in pricing, we feel it is highly relevant for understanding consumer judgments of "unfair" pricing. Forewarned is forearmed! Being aware of these moral foundations will prevent managers from getting blindsided by protests of price "unfairness." In particular, three of the six moral foundations that Haidt and his colleagues outline seem highly relevant for perceptions of "unfair" pricing:

- Violation of fairness/reciprocity norms
- Violation of ingroup/loyalty norms
- Violation of harm/care norms

Violation of fairness/reciprocity norms

According to researchers who study the psychology of morality, a major foundation of moral judgments is the foundation of fairness/reciprocity. This foundation is based on the evolutionary process of reciprocal altruism. Specifically, the fairness/reciprocity foundation covers norms of reciprocal relations, equality, proportionality, rights and justice. In terms of price "unfairness," when consumers feel that fairness/reciprocity norms have been violated, they are likely to think of the price as "unfair."

The basketball playoffs example involving the Knicks and the Heat fits in here. The mistake that the management committed is not that they charged a higher price for the later game (Games 1–4: $20, $40, $60 versus Game 5: $50, $80, $90). Rather, the biggest reason for the outcry was that the prices were increased *midway* through the playoffs. While consumers agree to the idea of paying higher ticket prices for the games in the playoffs (versus regular games), they find price increases midway through the playoffs process quite detestable. To avoid the fiasco the management simply had to declare the entire schedule of prices—for all seven games—upfront, rather than make changes midway. From the consumer's point of view it is simply "unfair" to change prices midway through the process—it violates accepted norms of fairness/reciprocity. Note that nowadays it is customary to declare the playoff ticket prices for all seven games upfront (if a game is not held then the consumer is refunded later).

Violation of ingroup/loyalty norms

Another important moral foundation is the idea of ingroup/loyalty. This foundation comes from our long-standing capability, as tribal creatures, of forming shifting coalitions. The ingroup/loyalty foundation covers moral obligations and considerations that come along with group membership such as loyalty, betrayal and expectations of preferential treatment. If a price increase or price difference is seen to violate ingroup/loyalty norms, consumers are likely to regard it as "unfair."

The furor over Amazon's DVD prices discussed earlier falls into this category. Recall that one group of consumers was charged $22.74 and another group was charged $26.94 for the same DVD. The damning verdict of price "unfairness" here did not stem from this price difference, as it is a mere $3.50 price difference. Rather, the price difference violated well-accepted norms of ingroup/loyalty. Specifically, the group that was charged a higher price comprised more loyal customers and the group that was charged a lower price comprised newer (and therefore "less loyal") customers. This set the "unfairness" alarm bells ringing as the prices seemed to suggest that Amazon was knowingly punishing loyalty. Of course, Amazon did not help matters when its spokesperson stated that it was a simple price test designed to determine consumer responses to different discount levels, and that the negative reaction was the result of confusion on the part of the consumers. This callous reaction only added fuel to the fire.

Note, though, that from a legal and economic perspective it is perfectly rational (as well as legal) to charge loyal customers (i.e. customers who have been transacting with the company for many years) higher prices relative to new customers. This is because it is entirely possible that loyal customers cost more to serve than new customers, and to make up for that difference firms need to charge loyal customers more than new customers. In fact, extensive research by Werner Reinartz of INSEAD and V. Kumar of Georgia State University has shown convincing evidence that loyal customers are often less profitable than new customers because they tend to comprise "high maintenance" relationships for firms. However, when it comes to "unfairness" judgments, customers base their verdict on heuristic thinking, not on careful economic considerations. In the consumer's mind the norm is simple: "It's simply wrong—immoral—to punish loyal behavior!"

Violation of harm/care norms
The harm/care foundation covers basic concerns about the suffering of others, including feelings of compassion and care. It is related to our

evolution as mammals with social attachment systems and an ability to feel the pain of others. It underlies the virtues of kindness, gentleness and nurturance. This is perhaps the most difficult norm-violation for managers and policy makers to placate. Once a consumer feels that a price increase has violated norms related to harm/care, it is almost impossible to convince him or her otherwise, even in the face of clear (and even unavoidable) reasons for the price increase.

The Tickle Me Elmo example we spoke about falls into this category. Truth be told, it is difficult to accurately predict the popularity of a toy like Tickle Me Elmo. It's not remotely akin to fast-moving consumer goods or durables for which very robust and reliable prediction models exist (recall our discussion of the Guadagni-Little model that is highly accurate in predicting adoption of fast-moving consumer goods). Reliable statistical models for predicting fads such as the Tickle Me Elmo are rare. In all likelihood, Fisher-Price truly underestimated the popularity of this version of Elmo. Additionally, since Fisher-Price does not control production (like many American companies, it outsources production to factories in China and Southeast Asia), it is difficult for Fisher-Price to abruptly ramp up supply and satisfy the pent-up demand. In fact, an extensive federal investigation revealed that Fisher-Price had *not* engaged in price gouging. Thus, here, the "unfairness" was clearly in the eye of the beholder. We believe that this incident involves a violation of norms related to harm/care. Consumers came to believe that Fisher-Price simply did not care about their welfare and was not compassionate about their needs (in this case, the special need for toys to be given as Christmas gifts to children). Once consumers perceived that norms related to harm/care had been violated, there was no turning back—no amount of rational explanation by the company could switch off the "unfair" alarm bells.

Unfortunately, Fisher-Price did certain things that further exacerbated the situation. For example, one of the reasons why consumers were loath to trust Fisher-Price's disclaimers is that the firm is a repeat offender. The problem of a wildly popular and high-priced Elmo occurred for several years in a row. There might be objective reasons as to why this occurred for each of the years when prices spiraled out of control. However, it is difficult for consumers to give the company the benefit of doubt when the issue repeats itself year after year—it is hard to ascribe away intent from repeat offenses. Additionally, Fisher-Price could have done certain things to shield itself from blame—things that videogame manufacturers, for example, regularly do. An Elmo-like shortage during the holidays also prevails in categories such as videogames. The lines for getting the new Wii or Xbox game tends to be unbelievably long. Their prices too go through the roof as demand regularly outstrips supply. However, videogame manufacturers such as Nintendo are able to shield themselves from accusations of price gouging by cleverly delineating their releases as "special edition" or "limited edition" offers. These monikers, albeit seemingly trivial, create an aura of natural scarcity that deflects blame for high prices away from the company.

Besides norms related to fairness/reciprocity, ingroup/loyalty and harm/care, there are three other moral foundations: authority/subversion (related to virtues of leadership and followership, including deference to legitimate authority and respect for traditions); sanctity/degradation (related to the psychology of disgust and contamination, which refers to virtues of living in an elevated, less carnal, more noble way); and liberty/oppression (related to feelings of reactance and resentment that people feel toward those who dominate them and restrict their liberty). However, we believe that a discussion of these moral foundations is beyond the scope of this book as violations of these norms are unlikely to trigger perceptions of price "unfairness."

Overall, it is very important for managers to keep an eye out for whether or not a proposed price increase (or price difference) runs the risk of turning into a norm-violating incident. Irrespective of whether it is a violation of usual-practice norms or moral norms, a norm-violating price is the first domino to trigger consumer suspicions of an "unfair" price.

Let's now look at a second domino that needs to fall in order to cement consumer suspicions of an "unfair" price.

Q2: Is the firm perceived to be responsible for the norm-violating price increase (or price difference)?

In the chain of reasoning that ultimately leads to perceptions of an "unfair" price, the second critical link is that of the firm's responsibility. This is the second question that managers need to ask themselves—is the firm likely to be perceived as responsible for the norm-violating price increase (or price difference)? If the answer to this question is no, then perceptions of price "unfairness" are unlikely. There are occasions when, despite the presence of a norm-violating price increase, a firm might not be held responsible. This might happen, for example, when a firm is forced to increase its prices because of changes in government regulation (e.g. mandated safety requirements for cars). This might also occur if the norm-violating price increase was unintentional (e.g. an electronic glitch at a reseller's website). However, if the answer to this question is yes, then suspicions of price "unfairness" are likely to increase further.

If consumers both (a) perceive the price increase (or price difference) to be norm-violating, and (b) perceive the firm to be responsible for that norm-violating price, they then start to look at the reasons behind the norm-violating incident. It is critical for managers to know these reasons because consumers' perceptions of price "unfairness" vary with the type of reason they think underlies the norm-violating incident.

Q3: What is the reason for the norm-violating price increase (or price difference)? Is it mitigating?

In the chain of reasoning that leads to perceptions of an "unfair" price, the third critical link is the reasons—whether real or perceived—that underlie the norm-violating price increase (or price difference). In short, managers need to ask themselves: what kind of reasons do consumers attribute to the norm-violating price increase (or price difference)? In particular, is it attributed to changes in quality, cost or demand?

Does it matter whether a norm-violating price is attributed to quality, cost or demand?

The answer to this last question is a resounding yes! When it comes to the reasons behind an offending price increase, not all reasons are created equal. Some reasons are more likely to make consumers conclude that the firm is being "unfair" in its pricing. Other reasons are much more likely to mitigate the charges of "unfair" prices. There is a clear gradient of culpability—the degree to which a consumer holds the firm culpable for an "unfair" price increase depends on the type of reason that is offered (or perceived) for the price increase.

Broadly speaking, reasons behind a price increase or price difference can be quality-based (e.g. "higher quality ingredients led to higher prices"), cost-based (e.g. "the cost of raw materials have gone up, so prices went up") or demand-based (e.g. "the product has become wildly popular and it is flying off the shelves; many more people want it than what the firm had anticipated, so prices are going up"). Quality-, cost- and demand-based reasons form an increasing culpability gradient, with quality-based reasons least likely to lead to claims of "unfairness" and demand-based reasons most likely to lead to claims of "unfair" pricing. Figure 7.2 expresses this culpability gradient in a schematic fashion, which we look at in more detail below.

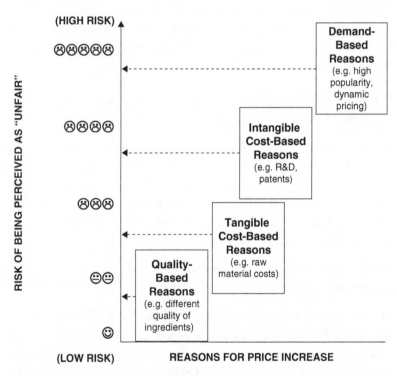

FIGURE 7.2 Risk of a price increase (or price difference) being perceived as "unfair" as a function of the reason for the price increase (or price difference)

Quality-based reasons

If the norm-violating price increase (or price difference) is attributed to quality-based reasons then it is least likely to raise the hackles of "unfairness." Consider, for example, two high-end hybrid cars, the BMW i8 and the Porsche 918 Spyder. While both are similar in terms of the eco-friendly attributes (e.g. miles per gallon, how long a charge lasts, emissions), the key difference is in the performance. While the acceleration from 0 to 60 miles per hour for the Porsche is 2.5 seconds, the BMW can only do 3.8 seconds. How much do you think the price difference between the two cars ought to be for the 1.3-second difference?

The BMW is priced at $135,000 and the Porsche at $845,000, a whopping $710,000 difference! Does a 1.3-second time difference justify a $710,000 price difference?

While a rational economist might keel over at this apparent injustice, most consumers will not be too perturbed. While the difference might amuse them or make them quizzical, it is highly unlikely that they will be up in arms about it. Many will simply say, "But a Porsche is a Porsche!" and attribute such differences to the super-premium quality of the venerated brand.

This is, of course, an extreme example. However, even in many relatively mundane purchase situations, the same rule applies—a price increase or price difference attributed to quality-based reasons is less likely to make consumers conclude that the firm is being "unfair," and consequently, is less likely to activate the STOP signal.

Cost-based reasons

Compared to quality-based reasons, cost-based reasons are more likely to lead to feelings of "unfairness." In the big scheme of things, however, cost-based reasons are relatively innocuous compared to demand-based reasons (which we will discuss in the next section).

In fact, it is not at all uncommon to hear that firms have successfully managed to pass on their cost increases to their consumers. For example, in November 2005 the *New York Times* provided extensive coverage of how a diverse range of firms, from airlines, hotels, restaurants, vehicle rentals, moving and storage services, and trucking, to manufacturers of fast-moving consumer goods such as soaps and detergents, over-the-counter medications, bicycles, kitchen appliances, boats and wine had managed to successfully pass on their cost increases to the end consumer. The price increases ranged from relatively small amounts (2.7% for airlines) to relatively large amounts (20% for hotels), thus allowing firms to successfully beat back the pressures of inflation. In all of these cases, the cost increases stemmed from rising raw material costs or energy costs. In short, consumers do not readily cry foul when they infer that a price increase was brought about by a corresponding increase in the costs of creating the product.

However, there is a small wrinkle in this argument about consumers' acceptance of cost-based reasons—not all cost-based price increases (or price differences) are treated alike.

The curious case of "intangible" costs

Consumers are less likely to protest against price increases that occur because of increased costs, *provided* those costs are easy to understand. For example, if an increase in the price of a pair of Nike sneakers is inferred to have occurred because of skyrocketing rubber prices in Malaysia (a major supplier of world rubber), the "unfair" buzzer is less likely to be pressed. Beyond these simple elements of cost, however, things get very hairy. For example, if cost elements are difficult for a consumer to fathom, even for completely subjective reasons, then the consumer is likely to deliver the "unfair" verdict and activate the STOP signal. Consider next, as an example, the case of a blockbuster blindness-reversing drug.

Paying for medicines that reverse blindness: FDA-approved?
No, I'll have the unapproved (and cheap) one!

In January 2006, after years of painstaking research, Genentech, a very successful drug manufacturer, launched a blockbuster drug, Lucentis, which was capable of reversing retinal blindness. Right from the word go the drug was a big hit, with its first-day sales registering $10 million, and its total sales in the second half of 2006 registering $371 million. Lucentis was priced at $2000 per shot, but experts noted that the price was well worth the improved clinical outcomes—patients' lives improved dramatically compared to any other alternative. Thus, for retinal blindness, Lucentis was simply the best possible, clinical-trial tested, FDA-approved cure.

Within a year of its launch, however, Genentech faced a very peculiar quandary. Sometime in early 2007, some doctors accidentally discovered that another drug, Avastin, seemed to have a very similar effect to Lucentis on retinal blindness. Accidental discoveries like these are often dismissed as flukes. However, in this case, there was a big reason to pause—Avastin, which was also made by Genentech, was priced at only $40 per shot! Patients and doctors started to switch en masse to Avastin. Charges of price "unfairness" or price gouging was levied on Genentech and there was even talk of a federal investigation.

Genentech countered these charges by pointing out that there were enormous differences in the costs of making these two drugs, clearly spelling out the costs that contributed to Lucentis' $2000 price and Avastin's $40 price. The company claimed they had nothing to hide and issued press releases that provided the cost break-up for the two drugs. These cost break-ups clearly showed—as verified by third parties—that the costs of manufacturing the two drugs were starkly different. In short, the cost break-ups fully justified the price differential.

In addition to transparent cost-based reasons for the price difference, Genentech also noted the safety aspect of the two drugs. Avastin was FDA-approved for treating colorectal cancer, not retinal blindness. Avastin had not gone through the same rigorous testing, via three phases of clinical trials, which Lucentis had been subjected to. Indeed, it had never been tested in clinical trials involving individuals suffering from retinal blindness, so its efficacy vis-à-vis retinal blindness was unknown. Moreover, its side effects from long-term usage were undocumented. Thus, in the absence of any objective data about its efficacy and side effects in 2007, adopting Avastin for treating retinal blindness was a very risky strategy.

Despite all these exhortations, however, the mass migration to Avastin continued. Consumers and doctors disregarded Genentech's argument. Both consumers and doctors continued to cry "unfair!"

Setting aside the question of who is in the wrong here—something that is yet to be resolved—this example poses an important question for our discussion of consumers' "unfairness" concerns. This example flies against our earlier claim that consumers are less likely to cry "unfair" when a price increase (or price difference) is cost-based. But in Genentech's case, despite millions of dollars spent on press releases, press conferences, public relations exercises and ads clarifying the cost-based reasons for the price differences, consumers continued to cry "unfair." What could explain this seeming anomaly?

The explanation lies in the fact that a lot of the cost components of these two drugs were difficult for consumers (and even doctors) to fathom—they were "intangible" costs. It was not a simple case of different kinds of raw materials (e.g. different kinds of chemicals) that contributed to the price difference. A large portion of the cost differential came from differences that are difficult for consumers to get their heads around, such as differential investment in research and development (R&D), size of the clinical trials (Lucentis used 6000+ clinical trial patients, considerably more than Avastin did), and the use of different manufacturing processes (Lucentis uses a more expensive bacteria production method). For a company such as Genentech these are, of course, very tangible costs! Often, decades of research and several billions of dollars go into developing an effective drug. But when it comes to "unfairness," objective reality doesn't matter to consumers—as we mentioned earlier, "unfairness" lies in the eye of the beholder. Perhaps with the rise of the Creative Economy, consumers will develop an appreciation for these kinds of intangible costs. However, as of now, the average consumer simply sweeps these costs aside. And as some astute pricing researchers—Joseph W. Alba (University of Florida) and Lisa Bolton (Pennsylvania State University)—have shown, even explicitly reminding consumers to take into account these intangible costs has very little effect in reducing their indictments of "unfairness."

These kinds of intangible costs can often land companies in trouble in terms of allegations of "unfair" pricing. This problem is quite common in many industries that have very high fixed costs (and low variable costs), or industries where intellectual property rights contribute majorly to the price of the good (e.g. from patents, trademarks, copyrights, legal and artistic fees). Arguments against allegations of price "unfairness," even if justified via costs, tend not to hold sway with consumers if they are based on intangible costs. As cases in point, think of the intractable problem of software piracy and illegal music downloads.

In fact, often consumers seek out "tangible" results in order to justify a price increase. In several studies looking at how consumers would react to an increase in the admission fees for nature parks and trails, or an increase in the tolls for certain roads and highways, researchers found that the public tends to be opposed to general price increases. However, the public is very supportive of a price hike if it is tied to specific projects or costs (e.g. adding or improving park facilities, adding highway lanes or rest-stop facilities).

Thus it is extremely important for managers and policy makers to distinguish between tangible costs (e.g. raw materials costs) and intangible costs (e.g. R&D costs). To the extent possible, managers and policy makers should emphasize cost-based reasons that are "tangible" and steer the consumer focus away from "intangible" cost-based reasons. Alternatively, if it is possible to frame an otherwise "intangible" cost in a more "tangible" manner, say, via clever ingredient-advertising (e.g. note the "Intel Inside!" campaign for Intel's processor chips that go into PCs and Macs), then firms should certainly attempt to do so.

We now move on to the third type of reason behind a price increase (or price difference).

Demand-based reasons

Of the three types of reasons, demand-based reasons are the most fraught with risk for firms. Demand-based reasons can often lead to complaints of "unfairness." In fact, compared to quality-based and cost-based reasons, demand-based reasons are significantly more likely to lead to accusations of "unfair" pricing practices.

It is not that consumers are unaware of how demand can lead to price increases. Consumers do understand that the price of a good can rise because of a rise in its demand. Most consumers have seen how more popular products tend to fetch higher prices in the market. They have an intuitive understanding of how, when there is a lot of demand for a product and its supply is relatively low, the prices will rise. Consumers also accept the economic rationale behind price discrimination—they understand that it is economically beneficial (and even appropriate) to charge different people different prices, in accordance to their willingness to pay. More recently, with the advent of yield management systems for airlines and hotels, consumers have also grown to accept prices that vary with time.

However, consumers' understanding of demand-based pricing is rudimentary and very vulnerable to their feelings of having being wronged. Thus, the business landscape is littered with examples of how demand-based reasons, often despite the best intentions of the company and despite being justifiable on economic grounds, led to accusations of "unfair" pricing. In reports of the Amazon (and other) incidents, *Washington Post* reporter David Streitfeld rightly remarked: "Few things stir up a consumer revolt quicker than the notion that someone else is getting a better deal."

Why do demand-based reasons, especially, not stick with consumers?

The reason why demand-based reasons tend to go awry more often than cost-based reasons pertains to the notion of responsibility. Cost-based reasons, especially those related to an escalation of raw material prices, can be seen as outside of a firm's control. Cost-based reasons are somewhat mitigating in nature—they shift the blame for "unfairness" to external forces. Consumers reason: "Oh well, it looks like it was outside their control!" Therefore, firms are seen as less responsible for cost-based price increases (or price differences).

However, the same cannot be said for demand-based reasons. Demand-based pricing, in most cases, is inexplicably linked to the idea of willful control. After all, demand-based pricing occurs precisely because the firm *willfully* charges different prices to different people, as well as different prices at different points of time. In fact, often firms are known to invest in resources (e.g. IT infrastructure) to be able to implement demand-based pricing schemes. Thus, when it comes to demand-based reasons, it is hard to make the case that the offending price increase (or price difference) was outside the firm's control. In the consumer's mind the logic is clear: "They're charging me a different price, simply because they *can* do so— that's unfair!" That is why demand-based reasons for price increases (or price differences) not only do not mitigate perceptions of "unfairness," but, in fact, they often exacerbate such perceptions.

In the section below let us look at some new examples, as well as revisit some old examples that we talked about earlier in this chapter. All these examples illustrate the frailty of demand-based reasons.

Coca-Cola's intelligent vending machine (and other dynamic pricing cases)

There is a simple economic principle that most people agree with—the price of a product should be commensurate with the utility that it provides. If a product provides more utility to the consumer at certain times (e.g. ice cream during summer) then it should be priced higher at those times compared to other times when it is likely to be enjoyed less (e.g. ice cream during winter). This is a demand-based pricing principle that most consumers agree with.

In keeping with this idea, in 1999 Coca-Cola started testing a vending machine that varied the price of the drink depending on the ambient temperature. Thus prices of Coca-Cola would go up when it was hot and would go down when it was colder. The logic was impeccable and Coca-Cola drinkers were already used to paying very different prices for the drink, ranging from 75 cents in a convenience store to $2 in movie theaters and sports stadiums. Doug Ivestor, the CEO, talked about the idea in an interview with a Brazilian magazine: "Coca-Cola is a product whose utility varies from moment to moment. In a final summer championship, when people meet in a stadium to have fun, the utility of a cold Coca-Cola is very high. So it is fair that it should be more expensive. The machine will simply make this process automatic."

The vending machine test was first reported in the *New York Times* on 28 October 1999. Consumer reaction thereafter was instantaneous, swift and brutal, resulting in a public relations fiasco for Coca-Cola. From newspaper editorials to online chat rooms, the denunciation was universal. Angry Coca-Cola drinkers complained of "unfair" pricing and cited this as an example of price gouging at its worst.

The problem with this vending machine experiment was not about logic or fairness in an objective economic sense; rather, it is a question of people's low tolerance for demand-based pricing schemes. If the fluctuations in the vending machine prices could somehow be tied to the cost of providing the service (e.g. how the cost of making Coca-Cola goes up on hotter days), the machine would have been better accepted. However, in the absence of any cost-based reasons, demand-based fluctuations in price are simply irksome to consumers and end up confirming their suspicion that the firm has been acting in an "unfair" manner.

Besides Coca-Cola, many other companies practicing dynamic pricing have also set off similar "unfairness" concerns. For example, an internet site varied the prices of a microwave oven from $744.46 to $871.49 in a span of a single day, and a children's apparel store changed prices every 15 minutes. In all these cases, there were extremely strong reactions from the consumer and complaints of "unfair" pricing were rampant. It's not that these firms were doing something illegal; they were simply implementing yield management "dynamic" pricing systems that are commonly employed for airlines, hotels and sports events. If these fluctuations in price could be tied to cost-based reasons, they would have created less of an "unfairness" furor. But the fact that they fluctuate so much in a single day, clearly rule out cost-based reasons from the consumer's mind. And once it becomes clear that it is an instance of dynamic pricing or demand-based pricing, then "unfairness" perceptions run rampant.

A very similar logic holds for the Victoria's Secret incident that we began the chapter with. Recall that Denise Katzman was incensed at Victoria's Secret for offering her colleague a bigger discount. Partly these allegations of "unfair" pricing stem from a violation of ingroup/loyalty norms. The customer was probably angry that, despite having been a loyal customer to the company, here was a complete stranger, even a male, who had got a better deal on the same product. Additionally, however, given that it was clearly a willful, demand-based reason driving the price difference, this further contributed to the feelings of "unfairness." If it could be attributed to quality-based (e.g. superior fabric) or cost-based (e.g. labor costs) reasons, the protestations of "unfair" pricing might have been less shrill. However, given that it was an identical product in an otherwise identical catalog, the idea of demand-based pricing or price discrimination was unavoidable. In the consumer's mind the logic is clear: "They're charging me a higher price, simply because they *can* do so—that's unfairly discriminating!" The judge presiding over the case ultimately dismissed the charges of "unfairness" citing that the ability to charge different prices to different people—what the market will bear—is a fundamental component of economic freedom and a market economy. However, as we have already argued, perceptions of "unfairness" are based on feelings of moral, not economic or legal rectitude.

Thus, it is very important for managers and policy makers to make sure that they understand what consumers think is the underlying reason for a norm-violating price increase (or price difference). Not all reasons for a price increase (or difference) are created equal; some, such as demand-based reasons, are much more likely than others—such as simple cost-based reasons—to set the "unfair" alarm bells ringing. Managers need to be aware of these reasoning-based differences in order to anticipate consumer reactions and design appropriate responses.

Now let's take another look at Figure 7.1 that lays out the chain of logic in the consumer's mind with regards to "unfair" pricing. So far we have looked at three critical questions that consumers tend to reason about: (a) whether the price increase (or difference) violates a norm; (b) whether the firm is responsible for the norm-violating price increase (or difference), and contingent on an affirmative answer to the question of responsibility; (c) whether the reasons for the price increase (or difference) mitigate the firm's responsibility.

But what happens when the firm is perceived to be *not* responsible for the norm-violating price increase (or price difference)? What if the answer to (b) above is in the negative? Is the firm then unlikely to suffer from perceptions of "unfair" pricing?

While firms might believe that not being responsible for a norm-violating price increase (or difference) should absolve the firm from allegations of "unfairness," the evidence points to the contrary. Even when a firm is objectively not responsible for the norm-violating incident, allegations of "unfair" pricing can persist. In the next section we discuss the specific conditions under which this might happen.

Q4: Is the firm perceived to have an obligation (and the capability) to prevent the norm-violating price increase (or price difference)?

So when is it that even when a firm is not perceived to be responsible for a norm-violating price, it can still be accused of "unfair" pricing? This can happen when the firm is perceived to have an obligation to prevent the norm-violating price increase (or difference) from occurring. The idea of obligation and capability go hand in hand. Consumers need to perceive both (a) that the firm had an *obligation* to prevent the unfortunate incident from happening (or shield people from the consequences), and (b) that the firm had the *capability* (i.e. monetary or other resources) to do so. For example, despite sharing an obligation, a small not-for-profit firm might be seen as less capable than a large corporation, and therefore, be blamed less for an "unfair" price.

Note, here too, the emphasis is on *perceived* obligation, not whether an obligation is objectively or economically warranted. This is a lesson that comes from, of all places, some recent natural disasters. Let's take a look at some of these incidents.

Lessons from Katrina: sure, the firm's not responsible for the hurricane, but it still feels "unfair"

As an illustration of the idea of obligation, consider what happened with gasoline prices in the aftermath of Hurricane Katrina in 2005. Clearly, gasoline firms were not responsible for the hurricane; it was an act of God. Also note that the hurricane did not appear out of the blue. It was expected, anticipated—and the post-hurricane damage was widely documented. In particular, newspapers, TV and other media provided extensive coverage of the damage that the hurricane did to the oil refineries along the Texas and Louisiana coasts. The fear was that extensive damage to these refineries, and their inability to refine crude oil and make it available for public consumption, would drive up gas prices. The media also set clear expectations that gasoline prices would increase. Not only that, they actually clearly declared, based on calculations by gasoline companies, that prices would go up by 50 cents per gallon after Hurricane Katrina. The prediction was accurate and post-hurricane prices went up by precisely the predicted amounts.

Yet, despite the fact that consumers did not perceive the gasoline firms to be responsible, and despite all the forewarning, there was widespread outrage at the gas pump. National and state level officials were deluged with charges of price gouging.

A federally mandated investigation (by FTC) into these charges of price gouging revealed no evidence (barring a few isolated instances) of actual price gouging. The charges of "unfair" gasoline prices, therefore, were truly in the eyes of the consumer.

Learning from the experience with Hurricane Katrina, a few months later when Hurricane Rita bore down on the Texas and Louisiana coasts, officials stepped up their efforts. This time a lot of media coverage and public alerts were devoted to the issue. The public was informed of the heavy damage that the hurricane had caused to the coastal refineries. The public was also told to expect a 20-cent per gallon increase in gas prices, a prediction that proved to be true.

Again, the same outrage regarding price gouging ensued.

And yet again, FTC-led investigations found that the charges of price gouging were largely unsubstantiated. The same scenario repeated itself after several other natural and man-made disasters.

These are clearly instances when a price increase is objectively justified. Indeed, some would say it is unavoidable—after all, the refineries were damaged by an act of God. Not only that, the consumer was even given an advanced warning about it and was told to expect a very specific price increase. So it is also difficult to argue that price expectations were grossly violated. Yet, the reactions at the gas pump were that of outrage and of having being wronged. Note also that when the media was carrying stories about this impending price increase, no one protested. All the protests broke out after the hurricane, when prices actually increased. Individual gas stations were widely suspected of price gouging. In reality, the charges of "unfair" pricing were largely false; consumers just *felt* that they were being charged an "unfair" price.

So what would explain this incident?

This incident is best viewed through the lens of obligation and capability. At times of crisis, whether natural or man-made, consumers feel that firms have a special obligation to help out people who have suffered as a result of a crisis. Thus, powerful firms are expected to shield powerless consumers from the fallout of such crises. Charging consumers a higher price under such extraordinary circumstances feels "unfair." This is what happened after hurricanes Katrina and Rita. Consumers felt that the oil companies had an obligation to shield consumers from the price increase, even though these companies were not responsible for the price increase. Moreover, oil companies with their deep pockets, were also perceived to have the capability to absorb the price increases and shield people. To consumers, oil companies seemed to be shirking their obligation despite having the financial capability. To consumers this simply felt unfair. Naturally, then, gasoline companies continued to be besieged with allegations of price "unfairness" despite not being held responsible for the price increase.

A similar thought process might also be implicated in the Tickle Me Elmo story that we discussed earlier. There might have been a segment of sophisticated customers who did not hold Fisher-Price, the makers of Elmo, responsible for the steep price increases. Perhaps they realized that there is no accounting for popularity of toys. However, even this group of consumers might have felt that Fisher-Price had an obligation, especially during a special occasion such as Christmas, to shield consumers from these price increases. Moreover, given Fisher-Price's size and reputation, consumers might also have reasoned that the company had the capability to bear the brunt of the price increases. These might have been additional reasons why consumer perceptions of "unfairness" were so sticky in the Tickle Me Elmo case.

Overall, the managerial takeaways from this chapter are clear. Managers need to be careful of price increases (or price differences) as they are often perceived to be "unfair" irrespective of whether or not there are rational grounds for such price increases (or price differences). Indictments of "unfair" pricing can be especially damning as they tend to amplify the STOP signal and significantly curtail purchases. However, there is a clear road map for negotiating this "unfairness" minefield. Managers can use the four questions that we discussed in this chapter (i.e. norm-violating? responsible? types of reasons? obligation/capability?) to reliably predict whether or not their proposed price will lead to perceptions of an "unfair" price, and the extent to which such perceptions of "unfairness" will be hard to shake off.

Yes, it is true that "unfairness" lies in the eye of the beholder, but having a clear map of the beholder's mind makes it that much easier to predict what the mind's eye is likely to see.

Credit cards and obesity
Small changes, big side effects

Since the mid-1980s, how Americans pay for economic transactions has changed considerably. Cash payments have been replaced by card payments. Consumers and merchants have embraced relatively painless forms of payments such as credit and debit cards. The average American today carries four or five plastic cards in their wallet to pay for their everyday transactions. In contrast, in the 1960s and 1970s most people paid for their purchases in cash. As banks, retail merchants and finance companies flooded the market with plastic cards of different color and design, people gladly switched from cash to cards because card payments obviated the hassles associated with cash payments: they no longer had to visit the banks or ATMs and stand in long queues to collect cash for their daily transactions; they did not have to worry about the possibility of running out of cash in a grocery store; and even if they finished all the cash in their bank account, credit card companies smilingly offered them money on credit. Never in the history of economic transactions has making a payment been as easy as it has been in the last three decades.

A scary correlation

Curiously around this same period, the average American's waistline has been going through a conspicuous transformation. It has been bulging noticeably. According to the Center for Disease Control, 34% of US adults are obese and an additional 33% are overweight.[1] This proportion has been steadily increasing over the past three decades. The statistics are scary. In 1990, there was not a single state in the United States where the proportion of obese people was more than 20%. That is, merely 25 years ago the proportion of obese people in each and every state was less than 20%. But in 2010, there was not a single state in the United States where the proportion of obese people was *less* than 20%. That is, in each and every state today, more than 20% of its inhabitants are clinically obese.

Numbers are usually dull and dreary and they seldom make a good story. Numbers typically do not have the power to emotionally arouse readers to action. But if you compare the obesity trends and the decline in cash payments side by side, you might feel a twinge of anxiety. The numbers shown in Table 8.1 have been pulled from two different sources— Surveys of Consumer Finances and the National Health and Nutritional Examination Survey—over a period of several years.

Obesity is a complex social problem caused by the interactive effects of various factors, such as changes in eating habits, changes in relative prices of unhealthy and healthy food items, and more sedentary lifestyles. So it will be far-fetched to attribute the obesity crisis solely to any one factor.

TABLE 8.1   Obesity and credit card ownership in the US

Year	% Obese or Overweight	% Having A Credit Card
1970–74	47	51
1988–94	56	70
1998–2000	65	73

Source: Data from (a) Surveys of Consumer Finances (1970–2000) and (2) National Health and Nutritional Examination Survey (1970–2000).

---

[1] Overweight and obesity states are determined by using weight and height to calculate a number called the "body mass index" (BMI). BMI is used because, for most people, it correlates with their amount of body fat. An adult who has a BMI between 25 and 29.9 is considered overweight. An adult who has a BMI of 30 or higher is considered obese.

However, the data in Table 8.1 does suggest that changes in the mode of payment might have served as a catalyst in the obesity epidemic. As the proportion of credit card ownership increased from 51% to 73%, the proportion of obese and overweight people in American society increased from 47% to 65%. This pattern of data suggests that the proliferation of credit cards might have something to do with the obesity epidemic. The proliferation of credit cards might have accelerated the effect of the social and economic factors that cause obesity. It might have added fuel to the fire. Did it?

By now readers—at least the ones who have been reading carefully— would be well aware that we do not infer causation from correlation. But such a scary correlation can definitely be the basis of a hypothesis about a causal effect that begs a thorough inquiry.

The Side Effect of Painless Payments

Do I have enough cash?

Forty-five year old Emma Abrams has always been a conscientious shopper. No one can accuse her of being a spendthrift. Quite to the contrary, some of her close family members often tease her about being stingy. She is always careful with her money. She feels bad when she spends money on unjustifiable purchases. In her circle of friends, she is never the one to walk into a shop and splurge on a beautiful dress or on an attractive pair of shoes on a whim. She compares prices across stores, keeps track of discounts and sales, and prefers to buy products only when they are available at a bargain price. That is a habit she acquired from her father—an intrinsic aversion to unjustifiable spending.

Emma has been the shopper-in-chief for her family for over 20 years now. Although her temperament has not changed, the way she pays for her transactions has definitely changed.

In the 1980s, as she set out for shopping, the first thing Emma used to ask herself was—*do I have enough cash*? This question was to avoid the embarrassment of being unable to pay the required amount at the cashier's register. Cash is a tangible medium of exchange. To complete the transaction one needs to physically carry the required cash. However, this seemingly innocuous question—do I have enough cash—necessitated by the nature of the tangible medium of exchange had some side effects on her thoughts and behaviors. To know how much cash one should carry, one needs to estimate one's expenditure. So when she used to pay in cash, she had to consider what items she might buy on the shopping trip, how much she might be spending on that trip and whether she needed to spend so much. These questions, in turn, influenced her mindset. They made her more sensitive to the pain of paying and the anticipated regret from spending money on impulsive purchases. These questions put her in a pain-minimization mindset and heightened her sensitivity to STOP signals.

However, in the past 15 years or so, Emma has stopped spending money in cash. With three credit cards—a MasterCard, a Visa and an American

Express card—and two debit cards in her wallet, there was no fear of her running out of money. At any point in time, in any part of the world, she could spend up to $10,000 without batting an eye. So she stopped asking herself whether she had enough cash. Of course, being a chronic spendthrift, she would never spend such an amount mindlessly. Nevertheless, the credit line and the instantaneous access to the cash in her bank account enabled Emma to let down her guard. She could relax her vigilance. This, in turn, influenced her shopping mindset. Even without being conscious about it, the change in mode of payment has subtly nudged her away from the pain-minimization mindset to benefit-maximization mindset. She started caring more about maximizing her happiness than about minimizing her pain. Compared to her younger self, she has now become less sensitive to STOP signals that rein in her impulsive purchases.

The irony is that she is not even aware of these side effects of the mode of payment.

Payment decoupling

Behavioral economists Drazen Prelec (MIT) and George Loewenstein (Carnegie Mellon University) argue that when people make purchases, they often experience an immediate pain of paying, which can undermine the pleasure derived from consumption. Just as the ticking of the taxi meter, for example, reduces one's pleasure from the ride, the pain of payment can direct attention away from the pleasure of consumption to its justifiability. Based on this premise these scholars argue that coupling between the pleasure of consumption and the pain of paying is an important determinant of purchase behavior. *Coupling* refers to the degree to which consumption calls to mind thoughts of payment, and vice versa. Some modes of payment, such as credit cards, tend to weaken coupling, whereas others, such as cash payment, produce tight coupling. When you buy something on a credit card, the consumption is immediate but you experience the pain of payment much later. In such cases, the payment is decoupled from the consumption and people focus more on the consumption pleasure than on the pain of payment.

In a similar vein, Dilip Soman, a consumer psychologist and professor of marketing at the University of Toronto, has argued that cash is the most transparent form of money because its status as legal tender makes it salient in both physical form and amount. When paying by cash, the feeling of parting with money is very vivid. Not just credit cards, in fact, but any other mode of payment that does not have the same emotional connection as cash can weaken consumers' STOP signals and lead to overspending. For example, people are likely to spend money more freely when the money is in the form of gift cards, loyalty points or cash equivalent certificates.

Consumer psychologists Priya Raghubir (New York University) and Joydeep Srivastava (University of Maryland) tested the hypothesis that not just credit cards, even other forms of painless payment will have the same effect as credit cards. In one of their experiments, some participants were given a $50 bill while others were given a $50 scrip certificate—a certificate whose value is recognized by the payer and payee. Participants then responded to a simulated shopping study. The researchers predicted that since paying by the scrip will feel less painful than paying in cash, participants will spend more with the scrip certificate. Consistent with their prediction, participants spent more when they were given a scrip certificate than when they were given an equivalent amount in cash.

Overlearned responses to cues

It is not just credit cards that can change consumer behavior—even credit card logos can change behavior.

Psychologists have shown that over time, people learn to associate certain behavioral responses with cues. Cues have the power to subconsciously trigger behaviors. Cash as well as credit card logos can serve as such cues. Mere exposure to credit card logos can direct attention to the desirability of the products being considered and strengthen the GO signals.

Richard Feinberg, a professor in the department of Consumer Sciences and Retailing at Purdue University, examined the tips left by cash and credit card customers in a restaurant. He predicted that for equivalent check amounts, credit card tips would be greater than cash tips. Consistent with his prediction, he found that mode of payment did influence the amount of tip. The average tip was 17% of the check when the restaurant's patrons used a credit card and only 15% when paid in cash.

Michael McCall and Heather Belmont of Ithaca College took this idea a step further and hypothesized that not just paying through credit cards but even mere exposure to credit card insignia can weaken the STOP signals and increase tipping. They ran their experiments in a restaurant in upstate New York. In their experiments, they manipulated the presence or absence of a credit cue on the tip tray. A credit card company provided tip trays containing its credit card insignia in the center of the tray. These trays were randomly mixed with blank tip trays traditionally used in the restaurant. Thus there were two types of tip trays used— blank tip trays and tip trays with a credit card logo. Some restaurant customers were given their bill in the blank trip tray while others were given the bill in the tip tray with a credit card logo. The researchers examined whether the mere presence of the credit card logo on the tip tray increased the amount of tipping.

It did. Those restaurant customers who received their bill on a tray that contained a credit insignia tipped a significantly higher percentage (20%) than those who received their bill on a blank tray (16%).

Cookies, donuts and fries

The research discussed thus far suggests that people spend more when they use credit cards. But is that necessarily bad? In fact, does not monetary flexibility empower customers to make healthy choices? For example, if a cash-strapped customer has access to easy credit, is he or she not more likely to choose organic lettuce and juicy apples over the less expensive doughnuts or pizza slices? At least that is what the credit card companies would like to argue: financial freedom leads to healthier food choices. So credit cards could actually lead to healthier consumption.

Does it actually?

One of the co-authors of this book, Manoj Thomas, along with research-ers from the State University of New York at Buffalo (Kalpesh Desai and Satheeshkumar Seenivasan) set out to answer this question. Using the scanner panel data from a large retail chain, they analyzed the shopping baskets of 1000 households over a period of six months, January to June 2003. This store keeps track of all the purchases of its loyal shoppers, how much they paid for each item, and whether they paid for the purchased items in cash or through credit or debit cards. In 2003, for these 1000 households, 41% of the transactions were done using credit cards, 9% of the transactions using debit cards and the remaining in cash (these pro-portions would have changed considerably today, with cash accounting for much lower proportion).

To examine whether the mode of payment influences the unhealthiness of baskets, the researchers computed an index of basket unhealthiness. They conducted a survey to get public ratings of unhealthiness of 100 popularly purchased food categories. Note that they were not interested in assessing basket unhealthiness using objective nutritional indicators. Instead, their interest was in assessing whether an average consumer *perceives* these food items as unhealthy. They wanted to examine whether shoppers are more likely to buy food items that they *believe* to be unhealthy when they pay using cards relative to when they pay in cash. Food items such as ice cream, candies, cookies, gum, donuts, potato chips and pudding were rated the unhealthiest in this survey. Vegetables, beans, barley and rice were rated the least unhealthy. Using these ratings, they computed an aver-age unhealthiness index for each shopping basket in the scanner panel data. They then examined whether the unhealthiness rating of the basket depended on the mode of payment.

Mode of payment did influence the unhealthiness rating of baskets.

Participants were more likely to either include unhealthy items or buy items with higher unhealthiness ratings when they paid using credit cards than when they paid in cash. Interestingly, this was true for debit cards as well: shopping baskets had higher unhealthiness ratings when consumers used debit cards to pay for them. This effect of debit card on unhealthiness consumption is intriguingly insightful as well as disconcerting.

It is intriguingly insightful because it shows that the effect of mode of payment is not based on rational considerations. Rationally speaking, paying using a debit card is no different from paying in cash. When a customer slides a debit card on a card reader and confirms the transaction, within a few minutes the money is moved out of his or her account. So a rational customer's behavior should not change depending on whether they are paying in cash or by debit card because for all practical purposes these two modes are identical. Yet, these results suggest that when it comes to the pain of payment, a debit card is similar to credit cards rather than to cash. Relative to cash, debit cards and credit cards are painless forms of payments. Both debit cards and credit cards weaken the STOP signals that curb impulsive purchases.

The fact that debit cards have the same effect as credit cards is not only intriguing, it is also disconcerting. More and more people are switching to debit cards based on the (mistaken) belief that by doing so they can regulate their spending behaviors more effectively when they use debit cards than when they use credit cards. This belief might be misplaced. In the mind's eye, a debit card is no different from a credit card. Both reduce the pain of payment and prime consumers to abandon their vigilance.

Vice and virtue products

Although the analysis of shopping baskets using scanner panel data suggests that credit cards can affect what people buy and eat, one cannot draw conclusive inferences from this study, because the results are based on patterns of correlations. The researchers found that, relative to cash payments, payments through credit as well as debit cards are more likely to be associated with unhealthy shopping baskets. However, such correlational studies are open to other interpretations. For instance, it could be argued that shoppers who are more impulsive in nature are more likely to use credit and debit cards. The more prudent ones would, a skeptic might argue, pay in cash. To rule out such alternative accounts, Thomas, Desai and Seenivasan conducted a series of experiments wherein they directly manipulated the mode of payment.

The experiment was rather straightforward. The researchers recruited some volunteers from an online forum to participate in a simulated shopping task. To prevent hypothesis guessing and contrived responses from participants, they were told that the study was run on behalf of a new retail store chain. The cover story was that the management of the retail store is doing marketing research to learn about shoppers' preferences for food products. However, unbeknown to the participants, they were randomly assigned to one of the two different versions of the study. Half the participants were assigned to the card-payment version of the study. In this version, the participants were told that the new retail store will accept all forms of credit and debit cards. This statement, displayed on the computer screen at the beginning of the study, was accompanied by the logos of major credit cards—Visa, MasterCard, Discover and American Express. Such messages are quite commonplace; most customers are used to seeing such logos as they enter a retail store.

The other half, chosen randomly, was assigned to the cash-payment version of the study. Participants assigned to this version were told that the new retail store will accept only cash payments. Note that since this was a simulated shopping task, the payments were notional; the participants did not have to actually pay anything. They had to merely assume paying for the simulated shopping either in cash or using cards. The researchers were interested in examining whether merely imagining paying in cash versus paying with a card would change their mindsets and thus influence their shopping basket in the simulated study.

After these instructions all participants completed the shopping task. The researchers used two different types of food products as stimuli in the shopping task—vice products and virtue products.

Vice products included items such as cookies, donuts, pies and cakes. Vice products evoke conflicting responses from consumers. On the one hand, some of these items elicit visceral GO signals in some consumers. The mere

thought of consuming these items makes some consumers spontaneously salivate, kindles their hunger and sets off an automatic "approach"
response. On the other hand, these items are also commonly believed to
be unhealthy. This belief triggers STOP signals that prevent them from
buying these items. Thus, for many shoppers vice products elicit conflicting emotions. The researchers predicted that purchase decisions of such
vice products should be particularly sensitive to small changes in pain of
payment; painless forms of payments should weaken the STOP signal and
increase the number of vice products in the basket.

Virtue products used in this study included items such as low fat yogurt,
cereal, oatmeal and water. These products are typically considered healthy

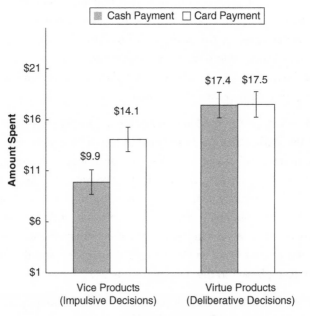

**FIGURE 8.1 / How card payments influence consumption of vice and virtue
products**

Source: Data from Manoj Thomas, Kalpesh Desai and Satheeshkumar Seenivasan (2011), How Credit
Card Payments Increase Unhealthy Food Purchases: Visceral Regulation of Vices, *Journal of Consumer
Research*, Vol. 38, No. 1, pp. 126–39.

and seldom purchased based on cravings or impulsive consumption urges. Most shoppers buy low fat yogurt, cereal and oatmeal after deliberative considerations. They sometimes consider the stock they have in their pantry, whether the price is attractive and whether it is on their shopping list for the week. Moreover, these purchases are completely justifiable. So these purchase decisions are not characterized by the conflict between GO and STOP signals, and therefore are less sensitive to the changes in STOP signals caused by the mode of payment. So mode of payment should not matter much for such products.

Figure 8.1 presents the results from this experiment. Merely imagining paying using a card instead of paying in cash increased the amount spent on vice products by around 15%. Participants in the card-payment condition spent $31.6 on shopping while those in the cash-payment condition spent $27.3. Almost all the incremental spending was on vice products. These results very closely mirror the finding from the scanner panel data study and confirm that credit cards can increase the consumption of unhealthy food items.

Counting without feeling

When we share these results in presentations and talks, one refrain that we often hear is: "I believe that card payments can increase unhealthy consumption for some consumers, but I don't think it happens to me. I always pay close attention to prices."

This argument is based on the assumption that credit cards lead to over-spending because people stop paying attention to prices when they use cards. The presumption is that if a consumer is very price conscious, then even when he or she uses credit cards they are likely to pay attention to prices. So their purchase decisions should not be influenced by the mode of payment.

However, research suggests that the card payment effect is not necessarily caused by inattention to prices. Of course, sometimes people might not pay close attention to prices when they pay using cards and this might reduce their price sensitivity. So inattention can sometimes cause the credit card effect. However, inattention is not a necessary condition for the credit card effect. Even when consumers pay attention to prices and track prices carefully, card payments can reduce price sensitivity by taking away the sting of payment. Parting with physical cash has a visceral effect. Taking out money from one's wallet and handing it over to someone can feel bad. Even the notion of parting with cash can feel bad. And it is this feeling that inhibits purchase decisions.

In contrast, when a shopper pays with a card, parting with money does not have that visceral effect. Price becomes a piece of cold information that needs to be compared and evaluated. And parting with money becomes an abstract distant notion. The money is not being taken out of your wallet; it is being taken out of some distant bank at a distant time. This mental decoupling of purchase and payment takes away the sting from transactions.

Decoupling of purchase and payment takes away the sting from transactions

To test whether this is actually the case, in one of their simulated shopping experiments Thomas and his collaborators did a surprise price recall test. Immediately after the simulated shopping task was over, they asked the participants to report the total value of the items that they had included in their shopping basket. The *actual* values and the values *reported by the participants* are summarized in Table 8.2.

Participants in the card-payment condition as well as those in the cash-payment condition were quite good at estimating the value of the items

TABLE 8.2   Shopper's actual and estimated spending

	Actual Value of Basket	Estimated Value of Basket	Difference
Card-Payment Condition	$28.5	$30.6	$2.1
Cash-Payment Condition	$20.7	$22.1	$1.4

Source: Data from Manoj Thomas, Kalpesh Desai and Satheeshkumar Seenivasan (2011), How Credit Card Payments Increase Unhealthy Food Purchases: Visceral Regulation of Vices, *Journal of Consumer Research*, Vol. 38, No. 1, pp. 126–39.

that they had included in the shopping basket. They could not have done so if they were ignoring the prices. Clearly, participants in both conditions were paying attention to prices. However, despite paying attention to prices, those in the card-payment condition spent more because they did not feel bad about spending the money.

Counting the money is not sufficient to experience the pain of payment. One has to count *with feeling*.

Public policy implications

As technological advances make our lives easier, the side effects and potential hazards also escalate. Alvin Toffler rightly remarked: "Our technological powers increase, but the side effects and potential hazards also escalate." But it seems that we, as a society, often ignore the side effects because they are hidden to the undiscerning eye. One has to connect the dots and see the big picture. And sometimes, one might even have to swim against the current.

There is too much evidence showing that credit and debit cards do now influence the manner in which we are spending money. It seems reasonable to argue that cashless payments, while much more convenient than cash transactions, might have been a catalyst in the growth of consumer debt in the recent decades. The data reviewed in this chapter also suggests that cashless payments might have been a catalyst in the alarming obesity crisis.

Corporations use consumer insights on a regular basis to maximize their profits without meaningfully caring about the side effects of their actions. They invest a lot of money in identifying deep-seated powerful insights that can change behaviors. Consumer insights not only drive their business strategy, but they also use these insights to influence policy decisions.

Here is one instance.

In the early days of credit cards, merchants used to charge a small surcharge when consumers paid by card instead of cash. That is, if a consumer paid by cash, they would pay the list price. However, if they paid using a credit card, then the retailer used to add a small surcharge—1% to 3% of the listed price—as a card-processing fee. This was legitimate because the credit card companies and the banks processing the credit card transactions took a small share of the money due to the merchants by way of a processing fee. But corporations and the credit card lobby soon realized that associating card payments with a surcharge was bad for their business. It would dissuade the card users from using credit cards and would instead encourage them to use cash. Paying an extra fee over and above the list price seems painful, and this in turn might serve as a STOP signal. Based on this consumer insight, the credit card companies tried to ban the merchants from charging a surcharge on card payments. When that did not work, the credit card lobby came up with a brilliant insight: it is better to offer a discount on cash payments rather than to add a surcharge on credit card payments. That way, credit card payments will look like the norm. They lobbied with the merchants and the legislators in Congress arguing for such a policy.

While corporations have employed astute managers to unearth and use powerful behavioral insights to maximize their profits, not many people are using such insights to protect consumer welfare. Who will worry about the side effects of the proliferation of card payments? Who will decide when the detrimental effects of card payments might outweigh the convenience of card usage? Clearly, expecting individual consumers to counter the power and influence of large corporations will be gross injustice. It is the role of government agencies, social and political leaders to address such issues and to create legislations and institutions that will protect consumer welfare and long-term wellbeing. Consumer insights can not only be used by managers and corporations, but can and should be used by government agencies to protect consumer welfare. Although a free market economy—where terms of exchange of goods and services are set freely by the forces of supply and demand and are allowed to reach their point of equilibrium without intervention by government policy—has been shown to be conducive to economic growth and creation of wealth, there is also growing fear that in the absence of proper checks and balances it could be detrimental to social wellbeing. While corporations fight with each other to increase their share of the market by developing innovative approaches to weaken STOP signals in consumers' minds and lure them to bite the bait, it is incumbent on the government agencies to monitor whether the STOP signals have been weakened to such an extent so as to endanger the long-term wellbeing of consumers. Therefore, leaders and bureaucrats in government agencies entrusted with public policy formulation have to be as well-versed in consumer insights as the astute managers running successful corporations. This chapter, and Chapter 7, highlight the importance of consumer insights for public policy decisions.

In the context of card payments, we highlight below two cases that deserve closer scrutiny from public policy formulators—food stamps and smart cards.

In recent years, traditional food stamps have taken the form of rechargeable plastic cards. Recipients of food stamps no longer have to collect and take the government-issued scrip to stores to pay for their provisions. Instead, they get a plastic card that looks and works like a debit card. All they have to do is to swipe that card at the store to pay for the provisions. There are numerous advantages of replacing food stamps with plastic cards, which is why the traditional stamps have been enthusiastically replaced by plastic cards. However, has anyone in the government agencies examined the effect of this change on the food consumption patterns of those who are getting the food subsidy? The research reviewed in this chapter suggests that paying for food items using such cards is likely to be less painful than paying through actual food stamps. Much like a dollar note, the food stamp is a transparent physical form of money and parting with money in such a form is likely to be salient. The same amount of money loaded on a plastic card loses its emotional salience. So when consumers pay using a card, they might be more likely to spend money on unhealthy food items. Though this hypothesis seems plausible and has serious implications, to the best of our knowledge, no one has tested it.

The second issue that deserves the attention of public policy formulators is innovative designs of payment cards to help consumers monitor and regulate their payments. Banks and corporations have invested consider-able money and effort to ensure the proliferation of payment cards and have ensured that it is easy to use cards for everyday transactions. But, somewhat surprisingly, the payment card is an opaque and unintelligent instrument compared to the traditional wallet. By looking into your wallet, you had some sense of how much money you have spent and how much you have available. But you cannot get any such information by looking at your bank card. This is surprising, because there have been impressive advances in real time connectivity and technology, and corporations have harnessed these advances to make it easier for consumers to use payment cards. That is, these companies made it easier for consumers to pay for the transactions, but not necessarily easier for them to monitor and regulate their cash flow. Not one major company, to our knowledge, considered it worthwhile to harness the same technology to create smart and intelligent payment cards that can inform consumers in real time how much money they have spent and whether they have exceeded their budget. For exam-ple, it does not take a genius to imagine a card with an embedded elec-tronic chip that controls a red-yellow-green color coding system to indicate the consumers' spending relative to their budget. If a red light turns on to alert a consumer that he or she has crossed their budget, it might not only lead to more prudent financial decisions but the pain-minimization mindset might also lead to healthier—or at least less unhealthy—eating habits. Although such smart cards are technologically feasible, corporations do not have the incentive to design and popularize such cards. Government agencies and public policy officials should take upon themselves the onus of developing smart cards based on actionable con-sumer insights and experimentation.

9

Why paying people to donate blood does not pay

Insights for public policy and prosocial behavior

The public policy arsenal: monetary incentives and fines

What has public policy got to do with GO and STOP signals?

Plenty, as the discussion and examples below—we hope—will show! For starters, many well-intentioned public policy initiatives suffer from the same hit-or-miss patterns that we described at the beginning of this book. The same monetary incentive or fine—two common weapons in the public policy arsenal—that worked wonderfully in one context completely backfires in another. Consider some incidents that exemplify this checkered pattern.

Monetary carrots: a hit-or-miss pattern

Hit. Governments have always used monetary carrots to encourage socially desirable behaviors. Providing monetary incentives has allowed governments all over the world to successfully encourage their citizens to buy hybrid cars, recycle plastic bottles and build energy-efficient homes, to name a few examples.

Miss—paying people to donate blood. It is critical to keep a blood bank well-stocked. Modern medical care would be handicapped without a well-stocked blood bank. Blood from blood banks is used not only for medical emergencies such as workplace or automobile accidents, but also for treatment of many chronic diseases and commonplace surgical procedures. At the same time, however, donating blood is an entirely voluntary act. Thus, public policy and government organizations have always worried about how to encourage this voluntary act in order to ensure that the blood banks are kept adequately full. For the most part, governments achieve this objective by exhorting people to donate blood through PSAs (public service announcements).

In the 1970s in the United Kingdom, and more recently in 2007 in Sweden, policy makers were considering increasing blood donation rates even further, beyond what regular PSAs had achieved. The organizations concerned decided to resort to a popular tool in the public policy arsenal—monetary incentives. Governments have always used monetary carrots to encourage a wide range of socially desirable behaviors. So why not pay people for their blood donations? After all, many people complained that they did not donate blood because of the "hassle" factor (time, money and forgetfulness) associated with traveling to a blood donation center. Surely, paying people some money to compensate for their "hassles" should only spur blood donations even further? It was this thinking that led the Regional Blood Center at Sahlgrenska University Hospital in Gothenburg, Sweden to offer people monetary incentives for donating blood. As part of a large-scale research initiative in 2007 the hospital offered each donor approximately US $7 for donating their blood.

The results were wholly unexpected.

Monetary incentives not only failed to spur blood donations, they in fact *decreased* blood donations at the university hospital. For certain demographic groups (e.g. women), the number of people donating blood dropped to *half* the usual number (i.e. the number of people donating blood when no compensation was offered). Thus, in this case, not only did the monetary incentive fail to have a positive effect on blood donations but it also, ironically, reduced blood donations. It backfired!

Monetary sticks: a hit-or-miss pattern

Hit. Governments all over the world have successfully used fines to curb socially undesirable behaviors such as drunk driving, littering and smoking in public spaces, to name a few.

Miss—fines for late pickups at daycare. Parents often pick up their kids late from daycare facilities. This is one of the most persistent problems that daycare facilities face. Seeking to address this problem, a classic intervention—deterrence via fines—was introduced in some private day-care facilities in Israel. In six of the ten daycare facilities where this study was carried out, the following deterrent message was posted:

> As you all know the official closing time of the day-care center is 4 PM every day. Since some parents have been coming late, we... have decided to impose a fine on parents who come late to pick up their children. As of next Sunday a fine of NIS 10 [about $4] will be charged every time a child is collected after 4:10 PM. This fine will be calculated monthly, and it is to be paid together with the regular monthly payment.

The remaining four daycare facilities served as a control group. The fine was imposed in the fifth week of the 20-week observation period and removed after the seventeenth week.

The researchers conducting the study—Uri Gneezy and Aldo Rustichini—found results that were very surprising.

First, the fines did not have any positive effect in terms of reducing tardy pickups by parents. In addition to that, surprisingly, the monetary fines actually backfired for the daycare company—the fines significantly *increased* the number of late pickups. More counterintuitively, the increased late pickups continued to remain at the new high level even when the fines were withdrawn in the seventeenth week. Thus, this was a case when a monetary fine not only failed to curb the socially undesirable behavior, but it also further exacerbated the very undesirable behavior that it was supposed to sanction!

What causes these policy hit-or-miss patterns?

Policy makers' approach to blood donations: the utility-maximization approach

At the heart of these hit-or-miss patterns is the standard behavioral framework that most policy makers rely on—the utility-maximization framework—in order to analyze people's behaviors and come up with interventions that encourage desirable behaviors and discourage undesirable ones. Within government and policy circles this framework is often referred to as the benefit–cost analysis approach, but for all practical purposes it is identical to the utility-maximization framework that we described in Chapter 1 (Figure 1.1). In order to understand better why this approach is responsible for the inconsistent patterns of success, let us first try to understand how a policy analyst would apply the utility-maximization approach to the socially desirable behaviors (e.g. blood donations) and socially undesirable behaviors (e.g. late pickups at daycares) that we have been talking about.

Under the utility-maximization approach, any given behavior of interest (e.g. donating blood) can be characterized as having two components: (a) the utility gained by engaging in the behavior (e.g. saving a life, helping others), and (b) the utility lost in order to engage in that behavior (e.g. travel time, waiting time, planning effort). As depicted in Figure 9.1, whether or not someone engages in that behavior will depend on the difference between the utility gained and the utility lost.

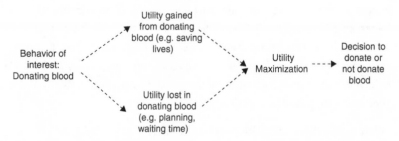

FIGURE 9.1 / The utility-maximization framework and blood donations

Figure 9.1 also provides a rough depiction of how a public policy analyst would look at the behavior of donating blood and go about proposing policy initiatives to encourage blood donations. Viewed through the utility-maximization lens, there are two levers of change that are available for policy makers: (a) increase the utility associated with donating blood, and (b) reduce the utility lost (i.e. disutility) associated with donating blood. According to this model, either increasing the utility or reducing the disutility should lead to an increase in blood donations. The policy makers in this case decided to go after the disutility component. The administrators at the Swedish hospital decided to compensate people US $7 for the "hassle" costs of donating blood, such as having to carve time out of a busy day, time and money spent traveling to the blood donation center and so on. Reducing the disutility associated with donating blood would lead to a more favorable utility-maximization calculus, increasing the number of people who would be willing to donate blood. From a utility-maximization perspective, the $7 initiative makes perfect sense.

But as we now know, not only did this initiative fail to increase blood donations, in fact it significantly decreased blood donations in some groups of people.

So what is wrong with the utility-maximization approach? And if it is clearly responsible for these hit-or-miss patterns, then which aspects of the utility-maximization model are especially culpable?

Why the utility-maximization model is a poor predictor of blood donations (and other behaviors)

The utility-maximization approach is an inconsistent predictor of blood donations (and other socially desirable and socially undesirable behaviors) because of at least two reasons. Both of these reasons are related to two faulty assumptions that the model often makes: (1) the policy–signal mismatch or discordant policies, and (2) the policy–signal side effect. Let's explore each of these in turn.

Reason 1: policy–signal mismatch or discordant policies

The fungibility assumption. A central feature of the utility-maximization model is to express both utilities and disutilities in monetary terms. Thus, even if the utility (e.g. added business activity on account of a new bridge) and disutility (e.g. time lost due to traffic snarls during the construction period) components pose an apples-to-oranges comparison, the model reduces both utility and disutility components to comparable monetary units. For example, the disutility of "time lost" above could be converted into equivalent monetary units by computing an "opportunity cost" of the foregone time (e.g. multiplying the additional minutes spent commuting by the average wage rate of the commuters). While this fungibility feature allows for easy comparison of utilities and disutilities, it lures the policy maker into lumping all types of utilities and disutilities associated with a behavior into one undifferentiated mass.

As an illustration, consider how the utility-maximization model treats all types of disutilities in a similar manner irrespective of whether those disutilities are monetary (e.g. the money spent on taking a taxi to the blood donation center; say, $5) or non-monetary (e.g. the cognitive effort of planning the trip to the blood donation center; say, computed to be $7). In designing "solutions" that would encourage blood donations, a policy analyst could advocate giving donors $7 in order to reduce the cognitive costs of planning the trip to the blood donation center. Said differently, a utility-maximization analyst could easily advocate a monetary solution to counter a non-monetary problem, and vice versa. This, of course, is not problematic in the world of utility-maximization models. This is because these models are agnostic to the differences between monetary and non-monetary disutilities, since, after all, all kinds of disutilities can be expressed in terms of their equivalent monetary units.

This fungibility assumption often leads policy makers to prescribe interventions that suffer from a policy–signal mismatch, one of the main reasons why many policy interventions are ineffective. Interventions tend to be ineffective when there is a "mismatch" between the type of the policy intervention and the type of GO or STOP signal driver that the intervention is supposed to address. The blood donations initiative failed primarily because there was a mismatch between the type of intervention (i.e. a purely monetary intervention) and the type of STOP signal driver (i.e. non-monetary "hassle" costs) that it was supposed to reduce.

The idea of a policy–signal "mismatch" is very similar to our discussion of "discordant" pricing in Chapter 6. In Chapter 6 we cautioned that if a manager's pricing strategy is "discordant" (i.e. does not match) with the consumer's mindset then the pricing strategy is likely to fail. In a similar vein, if a policy maker's intervention is "discordant" with the mindset of the people whose behavior the policy maker is trying to change, then the policy intervention is likely to fail as well. Thus, it is very important that policy makers avoid a policy–signal "mismatch," or what we will henceforth refer to as "discordant" policy interventions.

Note, however, that there is more to it than simply the monetary versus non-monetary distinction. To better understand how a "discordance" may arise it is important to know the different types of GO and STOP signal drivers. Let's look at these different types of GO and STOP signal drivers from the lens of blood donations and daycare pickups.

Different types of GO and STOP signal drivers. While many typologies are possible, it is especially important to distinguish between three categories of both GO and STOP signal drivers: (a) social drivers, (b) personal, non-monetary drivers, and (c) personal, monetary drivers.

Thus, when it comes to the GO signal, there are three distinct categories of GO signal drivers:

(a) *Social drivers of GO signal:* some GO signal drivers of a behavior may be social in nature. These are the drivers that motivate people to engage in the behavior for the larger good of the society, not for their personal benefit. For example, for the act of donating blood, the social drivers of the GO signal could be motivations related to helping others, saving lives, helping those in need and doing one's civic duty, to name a few. For the act of donating blood, the strongest GO signal drivers belong to this category. This is the primary motivation that drives people to donate blood. When it comes to picking up children from daycare centers in a timely fashion, the social drivers of the GO signal could be respect for social norms and wanting to avoid any inconvenience to the daycare staff. For timely daycare pickups too, the primary and strongest GO signal drivers belong to this category.

(b) *Personal, non-monetary drivers of GO signal:* some GO signal drivers of a behavior may be personal and non-monetary in nature. These drivers motivate people to engage in the behavior for the sake of personal benefits that are non-monetary. With regards to donating blood, these drivers could be motivations related to social signaling (i.e. signal to others how benevolent one is), or even self-signaling (i.e. signal to oneself how benevolent one is). For blood donations, a few of the GO signal drivers likely belong to this category (albeit far less numerous and less strong than the drivers in the first category). With regards to timely daycare pickups, these drivers could be related to not upsetting one's children, to avoid feeling a sense of shame and not wanting to experience a sense of guilt. For timely daycare pickups this category of GO signal drivers is likely to be less prominent than the social one.

(c) *Personal, monetary drivers of GO signal:* some GO signal drivers of a behavior may be personal and monetary in nature. These drivers motivate people to engage in the behavior for the sake of personal benefits that are monetary. With regards to donating blood, it is highly unlikely that any of the GO signal drivers populate this category. It is generally not a norm to get paid for donating blood. Even the Swedish example noted in this chapter was a one-off intervention; the payments were discontinued soon after the incident. A similar logic applies for timely daycare pickups, as parents are usually not rewarded for timely pickups. Thus, it is highly unlikely that potential blood donors or parents will be motivated by the prospect of personal monetary gains for these two behaviors.

In a similar vein, when it comes to looking at what stops people from engaging in a behavior, here too, there are three distinct categories of STOP signal drivers:

(a) *Social drivers of STOP signal:* some drivers of the STOP signal might be social in nature. That is, people do not engage in the behavior because social forces, whether real or perceived, stop them from doing so. Often this happens because people expect to be socially sanctioned (e.g. reprimanded, shamed, ostracized) if they engage in that behavior. For many behaviors that concern policy makers there are unlikely to be any social drivers of STOP signals. After all, no one gets socially sanctioned for donating blood or picking their kids up from daycare in a timely fashion. However, there might be some fringe occasions when this is the case. Consider for example, a person who might be worried about being seen as a "recycling geek" and standing out in a neighborhood where recycling is somewhat less prevalent. Sometimes this might also happen because people believe, rightly or wrongly, that the behavior is not good for society at large. Generally speaking, it is highly unlikely that a person would think that donating blood or timely daycare pickups is bad for society. However, there might be certain belief systems that lead people to believe otherwise. As an example, consider how Jehovah's Witness followers prefer not to donate blood or receive blood transfusions even in medical emergencies. Similarly, think of the sizable number of US citizens who do not believe in global warming and do not participate in efforts to minimize their carbon footprint. While these instances might be relatively rare, for a policy maker it is important to be vigilant to such possibilities. For the act of donating blood or timely daycare pickups, it is highly unlikely that any of the STOP signal drivers belong to this category.

(b) *Personal, non-monetary drivers of STOP signal:* some STOP signal drivers of a behavior may be personal and non-monetary in nature. For the act of donating blood these might be the "hassle" costs of donating blood, that is, the hassles of carving out time in the middle of a working day, the cognitive effort involved in planning the trip to the donation center, transportation costs, having to wait in line at the blood donation center, post-donation recovery time and the time lost in the entire exercise. When it comes to donating blood, despite the strong GO signals, it is these personal, non-monetary STOP signals that often get in the way. Most of the STOP signals related to donating blood tend to belong to this category. The primary STOP signal drivers for timely daycare pickups also belong to this category. Despite wanting to pick up their kids on time parents usually get stuck at work, previous meetings and last-minute errands spill over to the pickup time, or the pressure at work leads to momentary forgetfulness about the pickup time.

(c) *Personal, monetary drivers of STOP signal:* some STOP signal drivers of a behavior may be personal and monetary in nature. These drivers prevent people from engaging in the behavior because of personal constraints that are monetary. With regards to donating blood, it is unlikely that any of the STOP signal drivers populate this category. Generally speaking, donating blood is not an expensive affair. Certainly there might be potential donors who are so income constrained that the transportation costs and the opportunity cost of time spent in the entire blood donation exercise simply prevents them from donating blood. However, of late, the extensive use of mobile blood donation clinics has further lowered the transportation and time costs associated with donating blood. Thus, it is unlikely, albeit not entirely implausible, that prospective blood donors are being kept away because of personal financial constraints. The same logic applies for timely daycare pickups; it is unlikely that personal expenses are stopping parents from picking their kids up in a timely fashion. Note, however, for a different behavior (e.g. adopting a new, albeit expensive, "green" car), personal, monetary drivers of the STOP signal might be critical.

Now that we have reviewed the different types of GO and STOP signal drivers, let's go back to the two case studies and examine the nature of the "discordance" more closely.

The discordant policies for blood donations and daycare pickups explained

Figures 9.2 and 9.3 provide a bird's-eye view of the blood donations and daycare pickups case studies, respectively. Each figure highlights the key behavior of interest, the various types of GO and STOP signal drivers associated with that behavior, the relative importance of these drivers (primary, secondary, etc.), the policy initiative and the resulting discordance.

Both case studies illustrate that a discordance between the type of intervention, and the type of GO or STOP signal driver that the intervention is intended to address, often leads to ineffective policy interventions. One of the main reasons why paying people to donate blood was not an effective intervention is that there was a discordance between the type of intervention (i.e. the payment) and the primary type of STOP signal driver (i.e. the "hassle" costs). The intervention was purely monetary (i.e. cash payment of $7), whereas the primary STOP signal drivers were of the personal, non-monetary type (i.e. planning, travel, wait and other "hassles").

For the daycare pickups case study as well, there was a clear discordance. The policy intervention was a purely monetary penalty (i.e. $4 fine). In contrast, the primary STOP signal driver that it was supposed to deter

(The Action)	(Action Propensities)	Types of GO & STOP Signal Drivers	Type of Policy Intervention		
			Social	Personal, Non-Monetary	Personal, Monetary
Donating Blood	GO Signal (What drives people to donate blood?)	Social (PRIMARY) (e.g. helping others)	CONCORDANT	DISCORDANT	DISCORDANT
		Personal, Non-Monetary (Secondary (e.g. social signaling)	DISCORDANT	CONCORDANT	DISCORDANT
		Personal, Monetary (None)	DISCORDANT	DISCORDANT	CONCORDANT
	STOP Signal (What stops people from donating blood?)	Social (None)	CONCORDANT	DISCORDANT	DISCORDANT
		Personal, Non-Monetary (PRIMARY) (e.g. "hassle" costs)	DISCORDANT	CONCORDANT	DISCORDANT (e.g. $7 incentive in Sweden)
		Personal, Monetary (None)	DISCORDANT	DISCORDANT	CONCORDANT

FIGURE 9.2 / Monetary incentives for donating blood

(The Action)	(Action Propensities)	Types of GO & STOP Signal Drivers	Type of Policy Intervention		
			Social	Personal, Non-Monetary	Personal, Monetary
Daycare Pickups	GO Signal (What drives parents to pick their kids up from daycare in a timely fashion?)	Social (PRIMARY) (e.g. social norms)	CONCORDANT	DISCORDANT	DISCORDANT
		Personal, Non-Monetary (Secondary) (e.g. feelings of guilt)	DISCORDANT	CONCORDANT	DISCORDANT
		Personal, Monetary (None)	DISCORDANT	DISCORDANT	CONCORDANT
	STOP Signal (What stops parents from picking their kids up from daycare in a timely fashion?)	Social (None)	CONCORDANT	DISCORDANT	DISCORDANT
		Personal, Non-Monetary (PRIMARY) (e.g. office workload)	DISCORDANT	CONCORDANT	DISCORDANT (e.g. $4 fine in Israel)
		Personal, Monetary (None)	DISCORDANT	DISCORDANT	CONCORDANT

FIGURE 9.3 / Monetary fines for late daycare pickups

was personal, non-monetary in nature (i.e. work-related pressure and forgetfulness).

For maximal effectiveness, policy interventions need to match the signal driver type. If the aim is to reduce the STOP signal associated with a behavior, then it is important to make sure that a social STOP signal driver is countered with a social intervention. Likewise, a personal *non-monetary* STOP signal driver should be countered with an intervention that is personal and non-monetary in nature. Similarly, a personal *monetary* STOP signal driver should be countered with an intervention that is personal and monetary in nature. The same rule applies for increasing the GO signal associated with a behavior. It is important to make sure that a social GO signal driver is augmented with a social intervention. Likewise, a personal *non-monetary* GO signal driver should be augmented with an intervention that is personal and non-monetary in nature. Similarly, a personal *monetary* GO signal driver should be augmented with an intervention that is personal and monetary in nature.

For blood donations, most of the STOP signal drivers are personal and non-monetary in nature. These STOP signal drivers comprise things such as the cognitive effort of planning the trip, the travel time, the waiting time and other similar "hassle" costs. Rather than monetary incentives, perhaps non-monetary incentives that directly reduce the personal "hassle" costs of the individual might be more effective in increasing blood donation rates. An example of such a concordant policy initiative could be the use of mobile blood donation clinics that are located close to offices in business districts and kept open especially during lunchtimes and after 5pm when the workday ends. Similarly, if the aim is to improve the GO signal associated with donating blood, then paying people money should also be ineffective. Rather, it might be better to use concordant non-monetary interventions that amplify the social drivers or the personal, non-monetary drivers of the GO signal. For example, a highly visible, bright red sticker that proclaims "I just gave blood!" might work better as it strengthens the social signaling and self-signaling drivers of the GO signal associated with the act of donating blood.

A similar logic applies for timely daycare pickups as well. If the aim of the policy was to counter the primary STOP signals, then the intervention should not have been a monetary fine. Rather, concordant, personal non-monetary interventions might have worked better. For example, a "reminder service" whether through an app installed on the parents' cell-phones or via a phone call from the daycare staff, might have worked more effectively. Similarly, if the aim was to enhance the GO signals, then the intervention should have been social or personal, non-monetary in nature. For example, an intervention that enhances parents' respect for social norms (e.g. a sign that reads, "Join your fellow parents in being timely; 75% of parents pick up their kids on time") could have been more effective. As a case in point, consider how many green behaviors have been increased by invoking social norms (e.g. reusing towels in hotels increased by 25% when hotel rooms displayed a sign that read, "Join your fellow guests in helping to save the environment; 75% of guests participated in the towel-reuse program").

Why is a "discordant" policy ineffective? At this stage an astute reader might observe that the idea of a "discordant" policy merely tells us when a policy measure will be ineffective; it does not tell us *why* such "discordant" policies are ineffective. After all, an economist could argue: "Money is a fungible commodity. Why couldn't the potential blood donor convert the $7 personal, monetary payment into an appropriate defrayment for her or her personal, non-monetary hassle costs?" An extensive discussion of this issue is beyond the scope of this book; briefly, however, a "discordant" policy might be ineffective for two reasons. First, the policy maker might have simply gone wrong in his or her estimate of the monetary amount that would adequately counter the restraining force of a non-monetary STOP signal driver. For example, $7 might have been a gross underestimate of the "true" hassle costs of donating blood. Policy makers' best intentions notwithstanding, it is very easy to go wrong in such apples-to-oranges calculations. Second, even if the monetary incentive is appropriately calculated, a $7 monetary incentive aimed at compensating for the non-monetary "hassle" costs of donating blood assumes that the potential donor will appropriately "translate" the monetary incentive to its non-monetary benefits. Given that most people are "cognitive misers" such an effortful translation is highly unlikely to be undertaken or, at best, undertaken very imperfectly. To assume both that the policy makers will be accurate in setting the apples-to-oranges incentives, and that the individual will be accurate in his or her translation of these apples-to-oranges incentives, is taking the homo economicus assumption a bit too far. As we have argued extensively in Chapter 1, it is about time we firmly transitioned from the homo economicus model to the homo psychologicus model of behavior. Thus, when there is a discordance between the type of policy intervention and the type of signal that the intervention is supposed to address, it is not surprising that the intervention falls short.

Most people are "cognitive misers"

Besides a discordant policy, the second critical reason why many interventions fail is that policy makers fail to anticipate the side effects of their policy on the GO or STOP signal.

Reason 2: policy–signal side effect

Policy interventions are often designed to either increase the GO signals or decrease the STOP signals associated with a socially desirable behavior such as donating blood. Inadvertently, however, many policy interventions end up either dampening the GO signal or amplifying the STOP signal associated with the behavior. Here too, the key culprit is an erroneous assumption that the utility-maximization model makes.

The independence assumption. The other feature of the utility-maximization model that leads to the observed hit-or-miss patterns of success is the assumption that disutilities and utilities operate independent of each other. For a policy analyst using the utility-maximization approach, there are two independent routes to better outcomes. One could either attempt to reduce the disutility associated with the behavior of interest or attempt to increase the utility associated with that behavior. Reducing the disutility should have no direct impact on the utility and, likewise, increasing the utility should have no direct impact on the disutility. In short, there are no interrelationships between the disutilities and utilities associated with a behavior; the two are assumed to operate in an independent manner and each directly influence a person's likelihood of engaging in a behavior.

This too is an assumption of the model that leads to inconsistent predictions. As we discuss below, the two components—disutilities and utilities—are not necessarily independent. Often an intervention designed to reduce the disutility of engaging in a behavior might, perversely, decrease the perceived utility of engaging in that behavior. Similarly, interventions designed to increase the utility of engaging in a behavior might, perversely, increase the perceived disutility of engaging in that behavior. In designing policy interventions it is very important to take into account such interrelationships, otherwise not only do policy initiatives run the risk of being ineffective, but they also run the risk of backfiring.

The policy-signal side effect for blood donations and daycare pickups explained

Paying people money to donate blood dampened the GO signal in at least two distinct ways. First, paying people money might have dampened the social GO signal drivers associated with donating blood. The presence of a monetary payment demotes the act of donating blood from an act of pure "civic virtue" to a mere market transaction. This clearly dampens the social drivers of the GO signal associated with donating blood. Second, paying people money for their blood might also dampen the personal non-monetary GO signal drivers associated with the act of donating blood. Recall that some of the personal non-monetary benefits that potential donors derive from donating blood relate to social signaling and self-signaling benefits. That is, donating blood allows the donor to signal to the rest of society that he or she is a benevolent and magnanimous person. It also allows them to appear benevolent and magnanimous in their own eyes. By paying people $7 for donating their blood the intervention robbed potential donors of this signaling ability. After all, you cannot "boast" to your friends and colleagues, or even to your own self, about how you were nice and virtuous—because you got paid money. Altruism and monetary remuneration simply do not go hand in hand.

For the daycare pickups case, the fines inadvertently dampened the GO signal. In the absence of monetary fines, it was respect for norms, concern about inconveniencing the daycare staff, concern about social sanction and personal guilt that kept aberrant behavior in check. Fines, however, dampened these internal compliance forces. The fines dampened both the social (i.e. respect for social norms, concern about inconvenience to daycare staff) and the personal, non-monetary (i.e. feelings of guilt) GO signal drivers. The presence of externally imposed fines considerably weakened the internal social drivers. Also, "guilt" is a self-inflicted punishment for being late; the external monetary punishment substitutes for the self-inflicted one—you don't punish yourself twice for the same crime.

Note that this too is not a wholly new idea that we are introducing. The idea of "policy–signal side effect" is very similar to the idea of "side effect neglect" that we discussed in Chapter 1. The same mistakes occur in both consumer and public policy domains.

Policy–signal side effect is a major source of errors in the domain of public policy. Throughout this chapter we note many examples of how a policy intervention ends up having an unintended side effect. The blood donations and daycare cases are not isolated incidents. Note also that a policy side effect might occur even when there is no problem of a "discordant" policy. Thus it is very important for policy makers to carefully screen their proposed intervention for potential side effects as they might inadvertently end up curbing a socially desirable behavior and encouraging a socially undesirable behavior.

Why do policy–signal side effects occur? This is a very intriguing question. It is one thing if an incentive to engage in a good behavior does not work. But why would an incentive to engage in good behavior backfire and end up encouraging people to engage *less* in that good behavior? Similarly, it is one thing if a fine against a bad behavior is ineffective. But it is not entirely clear why a fine against a bad behavior would backfire and end up encouraging people to engage in *more* of that bad behavior?

Social scientists are still grappling with these questions and the reasons for these side effects are not entirely clear yet. However, recent studies using brain-scanning fMRI (functional Magnetic Resonance Imaging) techniques have brought new insights to the fore. In particular they show why, at a physiological level, these side effects might be occurring. These new findings further question the utility-maximization model of designing public policy interventions. We discuss these fascinating findings in the next section.

How the brain reacts to carrots and sticks: a delicate balance between external and internal systems

Public policy often deals with "compliance" behaviors. Many policy interventions are designed to encourage us to comply with what is good for society at large. This involves persuading us to engage in behaviors that are good for society and dissuading us from engaging in behaviors that are detrimental for society. From a policy perspective "persuasion" often entails a monetary fine to dissuade us from engaging in bad behaviors (e.g. late daycare pickups) and a monetary incentive to persuade us to engage in good behaviors (e.g. blood donations). In short, public policy tools serve as part of the "external" compliance forces that regulate and increase our compliance behaviors. However, "external" compliance forces are only part of the story behind an individual's overall compliance behaviors. The "internal" compliance forces matter as well. The "internal" compliance forces comprise an internal, self-regulatory mechanism that encourages us to comply with good behaviors (or stay away from bad behaviors) of our *own* volition. These internal self-regulatory mechanisms could be a sense of pride that drives us to engage in a good behavior (e.g. donating blood) or a feeling of guilt and shame that stops us from engaging in a bad behavior (e.g. picking up children late from daycare).

Naturally, then, an individual's overall compliance behavior will depend on the joint strength of these internal and external compliance forces. In fact, a rational economic model would assume that the external and internal forces are additive in nature. That is, an individual's overall compliance behavior is determined by the sum of the strengths of the internal and external compliance forces.

So far so good; this happens to be a fairly accurate characterization of the nature of the compliance forces that drive our overall compliance behaviors.

But what happens when we attempt to further increase compliance by increasing the external compliance force via, say, the threat of increased external sanctions or the promise of a reward? Does the overall compliance behavior go up? On a parallel note, what happens when we attempt to increase compliance by increasing the internal compliance force? Does the overall compliance behavior go up?

This is a very important question as a lot of public policy tools (e.g. fines, penalties, taxes, cash rewards, rebates) are aimed at strengthening the external compliance force that drives us. A central assumption in this chain of logic is that strengthening the external compliance force via, say a monetary reward or fine, will leave the internal compliance force unaltered. Similarly, it is also assumed that strengthening the internal compliance force will not affect the external compliance force. Admittedly, this is a fair and logical assumption to make, one that is made by the utility-maximization approach to policy decisions.

Unfortunately, however, new neuroscience research tells us that this utility-maximization model assumption is deeply flawed. This new research shows that our overall compliance behavior is made up of a delicate balance between the external compliance force and the internal compliance force. Attempts to alter one of the forces automatically affects the other force. Specifically, these researchers at the University of Zurich—Ruff, Ugazio and Fehr—find that these two forces act as substitutes. In other words, strengthening the "external" compliance force (e.g. via increased external sanctions) weakens the "internal" compliance force disproportionately, leading to a *decrease* in overall compliance behaviors. Conversely, weakening the "external" compliance force leads to opposite, compensatory effects on the strength of the "internal" force. In short, it appears that it is almost impossible to strengthen one of the compliance forces without weakening the other!

Let us look at this evidence more closely. Using fMRI brain-scanning techniques these researchers looked at how the brain responds to the threat of externally induced sanctions in a sharing game. Participants' brains were scanned while they engaged in this sharing game. In this game a participant was given a fixed sum of money, say $10, and had the option to share part, all or none of it with another participant. One key behavior of interest in this study was how much a person is willing to share with another participant voluntarily. The researchers referred to this as voluntary altruistic behavior. The researchers were also interested in how much the willingness to share would increase with the threat of external sanctions (e.g. the threat of punitive action by the other participant). So another key behavior of interest was what the researchers referred to as sanction-induced altruistic behavior. Thus, for each participant they obtained measures of voluntary and sanction-induced altruistic behavior. Since the fMRI brain scans were being conducted throughout the sharing-game exercise, the scans would tell us which areas of the brain are activated when participants engage in voluntary altruism versus sanction-induced altruism.

Past fMRI-based research has already shown that greater compliance behavior in response to external sanctions is associated with greater activation of an area of the brain known as the rLPFC (right lateral prefontal cortex). The rLPFC appears to be the "external compliance center" of the brain. In many past studies, the prefontal cortex region of the brain has been associated with impulse control and delay of gratification. Thus, if it was found that the activation of rLPFC is highly correlated with greater sharing in the sharing game (as opposed to keeping all of the $10 pie for oneself), it would have come as no surprise. Moreover, this kind of correlation would not establish causality.

Thus, these researchers added a special twist to their study. They went a step further than previous research—they directly altered the rLPFC activity via a safe and non-invasive method known as transcranial direct current stimulation (tDCS). Specifically, they randomly assigned participants to one of three conditions. In one condition, participants' rLPFC activity was not altered at all; this condition served as the control condition. In the second condition, participants' rLPFC activity was manipulated to be higher than normal, with the expectation that greater rLPFC activation would lead to greater compliance behavior. In the third condition, participants' rLPFC activity was manipulated to be lower than normal, with the expectation that lower rLPFC activation would lead to lower compliance.

In short, the key question that the study hoped to answer is—does ramping up the brain's "external compliance center" make people more compliant?

The answer depended on whether you looked at sanction-based compliance or voluntary compliance. For sanction-induced compliance the results were as expected. When the rLPFC activation was increased in participants, sanction-induced compliance (i.e. sharing $10) increased compared to the control condition. When rLPFC activation was decreased, sanction-induced compliance decreased compared to the control condition. Note that altering rLPFC activity did not change how punitive participants anticipated the other player would be; it simply changed their degree of compliance to the threat of punishment.

What about voluntary compliance (i.e. voluntary sharing)?

Here the results told a totally different story. Contrary to expectations, increasing rLPFC activation in participants did not increase voluntary compliance compared to the control condition. Surprisingly, not only did stimulating the rLPFC not increase voluntary sharing, it actually *decreased* voluntary sharing compared to the control condition. The empirical evidence showed a significant 33% drop in voluntary sharing compared to the control condition and a 41% drop in voluntary sharing compared to the decreased activation condition. Conversely, inhibiting the rLPFC did not inhibit voluntary sharing; rather it *increased* voluntary sharing (albeit the increase was not statistically significant compared to the control condition).

These findings are very informative for public policy decisions for at least three reasons. First, these findings appear to explain why sometimes policy interventions "backfire." We noted two instances when well-intentioned policy interventions not only failed to achieve their objectives but they also led to negative outcomes. Paying people $7 to donate blood *reduced* blood donation rates, and levying fines of $4 for late pickups at an Israeli daycare *increased* the late pickups. In each case, policy makers attempted to increase the strength of the "external" compliance force via monetary incentives or fines. What must have led to the lower compliance behaviors overall was a corresponding drop in the "internal" compliance force.

Second, these findings seem to suggest a piece of "bad news" for policy makers. Policy makers should note that any attempt to strengthen the "external" compliance force, whether through the threat of sanctions or through the promise of rewards, is highly likely to lead to a significant drop in the "internal" compliance force. This clearly runs the risk of rendering the policy intervention ineffective. Additionally, if this drop in the "internal" compliance force is *disproportionate*, then it also runs the risk of backfiring and reducing compliance behaviors overall. In this case, the policy intervention makes things worse—the world would have been better off without it!

Third, these findings seem to offer a second piece of "bad news" for policy makers. It is quite clear that attempting to strengthen the external compliance force significantly weakens the internal compliance force. But what happens when we weaken the "external" compliance force? Does it not increase the "internal" compliance force? In short, as a solution to the first piece of bad news above, a policy maker could easily suggest: "Can't we then just take away the external sanctions and rewards and restore the balance?"

Unfortunately, the findings suggest otherwise. While it is true that strengthening the "external" compliance force weakens the "internal" compliance force—and weakening the "external" compliance force strengthens the "internal" compliance force—there appears to be an asymmetry in the strength of the two effects. The former effect is much stronger; the latter effect is much weaker and, as we noted earlier, it is not statistically significant. Thus, while taking away external sanctions will indeed increase the internal compliance force, unfortunately, this increase might not be significant. In fact, a piece of the findings from the Israeli daycare case study seems to confirm this. Recall that even when the fines were lifted in the seventeenth week, the late pickups continued to remain at the new high level throughout the rest of the 20-week observation period. Thus, lifting the sanctions did not restore the balance and late pickups continued to occur at the new high rates.

Taken together, these findings appear to suggest a double whammy— damned if you do (i.e. strengthen the external), damned if you don't (i.e. take away the external compliance force). Robert Sapolsky, a renowned professor of neurology, neurological sciences and neurosurgery at Stanford University, reviewed these findings. His remark best captures these findings: "[the brain] … can't simultaneously prompt you to do the right thing because it's the right thing and because otherwise you're going to get your butt kicked."

A "side effect" can occur without a "discordant" policy: voting in Switzerland

In this section we discuss a case study on voting behavior in Switzerland. This case is instructive for a couple of reasons. One, it further underscores the importance of looking out for policy–signal side effects, by showing that a side effect can occur even when there is no "discordance" between the type of policy intervention and the type of signal that the intervention is aimed at. Two, it shows that it is not just monetary incentives and monetary fines that backfire, even non-monetary policy interventions can backfire.

Hit. Making it easy for consumers to order products and services from the convenience and comfort of their homes has increased consumer participation in the marketplace and led to the success of several online giants such as Amazon, eBay and Fresh Direct, to name a few. From a policy-making perspective, innovations such as e-file (the US government's online portal for filing taxes) have led to an increase in timely tax compliance. In each of these cases the convenience of being able to perform an activity from home, at any time of one's choosing, increased people's ability to success-fully complete the task.

Miss—making it "easy" for people to vote. George Jean Nathan once warned us: "Bad officials are elected by good citizens who do not vote." Despite his now famous admonishment, however, most people don't vote. It's not just a question of good citizens; citizens across the board simply do not vote in high enough numbers. According to the bipartisan Pew Research Center in the 2012 US Congressional Elections only 37% of the voting-age population voted. Even the highly anticipated presidential elections in 2012 saw a turnout of only 54%. Thus increasing voter turn-out has been a top priority for public policy officials in the US, as well as for officials in other countries such as Switzerland, which suffers from a similar problem.

In Switzerland, in particular, public policy officials were worried. Voter turnout was experiencing an inexorable downward spiral, down from approximately an 85% turnout in 1951 to a 55% turnout in 1977. In order to counter this worrisome trend, policy makers decided to make it "easier" for voters to cast their votes. When voters were asked why they did not vote, many cited the "hassle" factor associated with voting—the hassles of having to carve some time out of one's busy schedule, travel to a polling booth, spend time waiting in a queue and so on. The policy makers crafted a "convenient" solution—a postal ballot system—that would allow people to vote from their homes in a safe, secure and comfortable manner. The plan was gradually rolled out in Switzerland's 26 cantons from the 1980s till the 1990s.

The standard, utility-maximization expectation was quite simple. Voting, like any other activity, comprises a bundle of utilities (e.g. electing the candidate of one's choice) and disutilities (e.g. time and effort required to go to the polling station). A person's decision regarding whether or not they should go out and cast their vote depends on a careful consideration of these potential utilities and disutilities. If the potential utility outweighs the disutility, a high turnout is likely. However, if the disutility dwarfs the potential utility, a low turnout is likely. Naturally, then, lowering the "hassle" costs of voting, like the Swiss authorities had done, was expected to significantly increase voter turnout in Switzerland.

However, in sharp contrast to the utility-maximization expectation outlined above, allowing people to cast their votes from the convenience of their homes did not increase voter turnout. In fact, there is strong evidence that the postal voting initiative even backfired. Ironically, the presence of a home-based voting system significantly *reduced* voter turnout in Swiss cantonal elections (e.g. Zurich and St Gallen cantons) from 1991 to 1999.

Note that the postal ballot system was an *additional option* that voters could resort to—they were not restricted to a postal ballot system alone. They were free to walk to a polling station to cast their vote in person, if they disliked casting their vote via postal ballot. So it is not the case that the voter's freedom to cast their vote in person was taken away by this initiative. The postal ballot initiative truly made it easier for the Swiss voting-age population to vote. Despite that, voter turnout did not increase and in many instances actually decreased. Thus, this was a case where a non-monetary incentive not only failed to aid and abet the socially desirable behavior that it was supposed to encourage, but it also ended up discouraging that socially desirable behavior. In short, it is likely that Swiss voter turnout would have been higher had the policy makers not taken this (irreversible) initiative!

Why did this non-monetary intervention fail?

Figure 9.4 provides a bird's-eye view of the Swiss voter turnout case study. What are the GO signal drivers of voting—what drives people to go out and cast their vote? Some GO signal drivers are social in nature. People vote because they want to make a difference, determine the outcome of the election, elect appropriate leaders, and because it is their civic and moral duty to do so. There are also some strong GO signal drivers that are personal, non-monetary in nature, such as wanting to signal one's "civic virtue" to others. Note that many social scientists argue that the idea of making a difference, or determining the outcome of an election, has more to do with perceptions than objective reality. After all, a single vote is highly unlikely to be either influential or deterministic in most elections. Given this, many social scientists argue that the personal, non-monetary drivers of the GO signal associated with voting (i.e. signaling one's civic virtue) are stronger than their purely social counterparts (i.e. making a difference). Whether one of these drivers is truly stronger than the other, is, of course, open to debate. However, for the purposes of our discussion it would be safe to assume that both these types of GO signal drivers are equally prominent in driving voter turnout. There are unlikely to be any personal, monetary drivers of the GO signal, as we are usually not monetarily compensated for voting.

Now let's look at the STOP signal drivers of voting—what stops people from going out and casting their vote? There are usually no social STOP signal drivers, as there is unlikely to be any social sanctions against voting. Rather, most of the STOP signal drivers tend to be personal, non-monetary in nature. There are a lot of "hassle" costs involved in voting, such as the planning effort, the time and transportation costs involved in traveling to the polling station, and time spent waiting in the queue at the polling station. There are unlikely to be any STOP signal drivers that are personal, monetary in nature, as casting a vote is simply not an expensive affair.

Having looked at the GO and STOP signal drivers it becomes apparent that there is one main reason why the policy intervention failed. Note that there was no policy "discordance" as both the policy intervention (i.e. postal ballots) and the STOP signal driver (i.e. "hassle" costs of voting) were of the personal, non-monetary type. Rather, the intervention ran into problems with side effects. The policy tool inadvertently ended up dampening the GO signal. The "convenience" of voting from home robbed people of their ability to send out social signals of their sense of civic responsibility. It is difficult to display one's "civic virtue" in private.

If you are not fully convinced about the lure of signaling when it comes to voting, just type in the words "India voting ink" in Google (or any search engine) and do an image search. From the search results you will see Indians

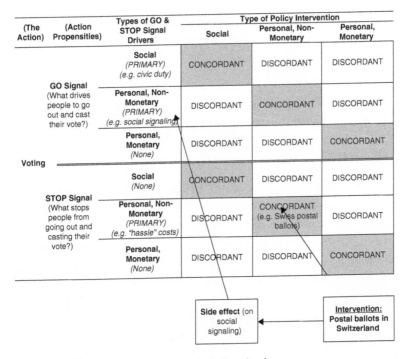

(The Action)	(Action Propensities)	Types of GO & STOP Signal Drivers	Type of Policy Intervention		
			Social	Personal, Non-Monetary	Personal, Monetary
Voting	GO Signal (What drives people to go out and cast their vote?)	Social (PRIMARY) (e.g. civic duty)	CONCORDANT	DISCORDANT	DISCORDANT
		Personal, Non-Monetary (PRIMARY) (e.g. social signaling)	DISCORDANT	CONCORDANT	DISCORDANT
		Personal, Monetary (None)	DISCORDANT	DISCORDANT	CONCORDANT
	STOP Signal (What stops people from going out and casting their vote?)	Social (None)	CONCORDANT	DISCORDANT	DISCORDANT
		Personal, Non-Monetary (PRIMARY) (e.g. "hassle" costs)	DISCORDANT	CONCORDANT (e.g. Swiss postal ballots)	DISCORDANT
		Personal, Monetary (None)	DISCORDANT	DISCORDANT	CONCORDANT

Side effect (on social signaling)

Intervention: Postal ballots in Switzerland

FIGURE 9.4 / Making it "easy" to vote in Switzerland

from all walks of life—from farmers, villagers and middle-class citizens to movie stars, cricket players, business tycoons and politicians—proudly holding up their "ink stained" index finger to the camera. It is their way of proudly proclaiming their civic virtue. This "electoral ink" is a semi-permanent dark-blue ink or dye, which is applied to the index finger of voters during elections. Its primary purpose is to prevent electoral fraud such as double voting, especially in countries where identification documents for citizens are not always standardized or institutionalized. However, what was originally designed purely as a fraud protection mechanism has now transformed into a "badge of honor" that voters in India (and in many other countries) proudly display and simply cannot do without. The signaling-related benefits from voting are not trivial and can be quite powerful. Thus, it is not surprising that the Swiss policy intervention not only failed to increase voter turnout, but it also ended up decreasing voter turnout.

Enough said about public policy failures; let's now look at some recent public policy success stories. Readers will notice a common theme running through all of these success stories.

Successful policy interventions: a tale of concordant policies and no side effects

The "Cash for Clunkers" program in the US

We have spoken at length about the failure of monetary incentives (e.g. blood donations in Switzerland) and monetary fines (e.g. daycare pickups in Israel). However, we don't want to leave readers with the mistaken assumption that monetary incentives are a bad idea. It really depends on the "match"—a monetary incentive will be effective if the key STOP signal driver is also monetary in nature. In other words, just as "discordant" policies tend to fail, "concordant" policies tend to succeed. The "Cash for Clunkers" program in the US, a program that incentivizes people to switch to greener cars, is a case in point. Figure 9.5 describes this case study.

Let's begin by looking at the GO signal drivers—what drives people to buy greener cars? Many GO signal drivers are social in nature, such as concern for the environment, doing one's bit to reduce global warming and respect for social norms. These are likely to be the primary GO signal drivers. There are also GO signal drivers that are personal, non-monetary in nature, such as wanting to signal one's "greenness" to others. This category is likely of secondary importance. There are also personal, monetary drivers of the GO signal, as greener cars lower gasoline bills. These savings, however, materialize in the long run. Consequently, this category is also likely to be of secondary importance.

Now let's look at the STOP signal drivers—what stops people from buying greener cars? There are no social STOP signal drivers, as there are no social sanctions against buying greener cars. There are also a few STOP signal drivers that are personal, non-monetary in nature, like the effort and planning required to switch one's older car (or "clunker") for a newer, greener car. This category is likely to be of secondary importance. The most significant STOP signal drivers, however, are personal, monetary in nature. Despite all the advances in technology, a greener car still costs more to buy. By some estimates a hybrid car costs anywhere between $2000 and $7000 more than comparable non-hybrid cars. While it is true that this price difference is, in the long run, more than made up by the lower fuel consumption, we know that consumers usually eschew the long term. The "sticker shock" snuffs out any possibility of long-term reasoning. The "cash for clunkers" program was directly aimed at addressing this—significant cash incentives were provided for car owners to trade in their older cars for newer, more fuel-efficient cars.

The program was very successful in making people switch to greener cars. In less than a year 690,114 dealer transactions were conducted. The average fuel efficiency of trade-ins was 15.8 miles per gallon (mpg), compared

(The Action)	(Action Propensities)	Types of GO & STOP Signal Drivers	Type of Policy Intervention		
			Social	Personal, Non-Monetary	Personal, Monetary
Greener Cars	GO Signal (What drives people to buy greener cars?)	Social (PRIMARY) (e.g. concern for environment)	CONCORDANT	DISCORDANT	DISCORDANT
		Personal, Non-Monetary (Secondary) (e.g. social signaling)	DISCORDANT	CONCORDANT	DISCORDANT
		Personal, Monetary (Secondary) (e.g. law gas bills)	DISCORDANT	DISCORDANT	CONCORDANT
	STOP Signal (What stops people from buying greener cars?)	Social (None)	CONCORDANT	DISCORDANT	DISCORDANT
		Personal, Non-Monetary (Secondary) (e.g. "hassle" of changing cars)	DISCORDANT	CONCORDANT	DISCORDANT
		Personal, Monetary (PRIMARY) (e.g. higher price)	DISCORDANT	DISCORDANT	CONCORDANT (e.g. "Cash for Clunkers" in US)

FIGURE 9.5 / Monetary incentives ("cash for clunkers") for greener cars

to 24.9 mpg for the new cars purchased to replace them, translating to a 58% improvement in fuel efficiency.

Having looked at the details of the case it becomes clear that the intervention succeeded because there was a clear concordance between the policy tool (i.e. cash rebates) and the type of STOP signal driver (i.e. high price) that it was designed to lower. Both were of the personal, monetary type. Additionally, there were no side effects. Thus, cash incentives can also succeed—there just needs to be a presence of "concordance" and an absence of "side effects."

Encouraging green behaviors

Many green behaviors such as not using plastic bags, reusing hotel towels, using fans along with air conditioners and so on involve making small changes to otherwise strongly ingrained habits. They do not involve high monetary or social costs, yet these behaviors have proven difficult to change for the better, even with steep fines or promising rewards. More recent research, however, has shown us how to achieve success in changing these "low cost" green behaviors for the better.

In large part these recent successes stem from the fact that researchers have moved away from monetary deterrence (i.e. fines) and encouragement (i.e. rebates, cash incentives). They have achieved much better success using non-monetary interventions. In hindsight this is not surprising. If you think about these low-cost green behaviors—not using plastic bags, reusing hotel towels, using fans instead of air conditioners, watering lawns less and efficient-energy consumption at home, to name a few—the strongest GO and STOP signal drivers are either of the social type or of the personal, non-monetary type. For example, the primary GO signal drivers are of the social kind, wherein people's concern for the environment, their willingness to do their bit to reduce global warming and respect for social norms prompt them to be greener. Some secondary GO signal drivers are also personal, non-monetary in nature, as some people might want to signal their "greenness" to others. Similarly, the primary STOP signal drivers are of the personal, non-monetary type, as the inertia of our old habits and the hassle costs of inculcating new habits get in the way of being greener. Naturally, then, monetary interventions (e.g. fines or rewards) are likely to be ineffective in either decreasing the STOP signals or increasing the GO signals associated with these behaviors. What are likely to succeed are "concordant" non-monetary interventions that either (a) amplify the primary GO signal drivers, or (b) dampen the primary STOP signal drivers. This is exactly what happened in each of these cases below. Let's take a look at these interesting cases.

Not using plastic bags

Effective 1 January 2010, Washington, DC imposed a five-cent tax on every plastic bag handed out at food, liquor and candy retailers in the city. However, what really tipped the scales was not this nominal tax—after all, it's a five-cent tax—but that plastic bags were no longer the "default" at retail stores. Cashiers and baggers at grocery stores would not automatically place the purchases into a plastic bag. If a customer wanted a plastic bag then he or she had to ask the cashier for one. Having to publicly ask for a landfill-nightmare plastic bag in front of other people made a big difference to usage of plastic bags in DC. The use of plastic bags went down, compared to previous years, by 11 million in the first quarter and by 13 million in the second quarter of 2010. No wonder during the annual Potomac River Watershed Cleanup day in April 2010, volunteers found 66% fewer plastic bags compared to the previous year.

This was an ingenious idea. What stops us from not using plastic bags (or using paper or reusable bags)? The biggest drivers of the STOP signal here are personal, non-monetary in nature. We are creatures of old habits and it takes too much cognitive effort to change our ways. Removing plastic bags as the default option was a good way to jolt us out of our inertial indolence. Additionally, having to ask for plastic bags in front of everyone else threatened to take away our green credentials publicly. Both these non-monetary interventions—leveraging the power of social norms and peer pressure—significantly reduced the personal, non-monetary STOP signals and succeeded in getting people to not use plastic bags. Whether this success will continue into the future, or for that matter whether it will result in a "rebound" that leads to an overconsumption of paper and reusable bags, is a different matter altogether.

Reusing towels in hotels

We have seen this message countless times in hotel bathrooms, imploring us to consider reusing the towels (instead of them being laundered after a single use). It's a simple and easy-to-fulfill request, yet we often ignore it despite the environmental consequences. Imploring hotel guests to "Help Save the Environment" or urging them to "Show Your Respect for Nature" did not have much effect. What did have a big effect was a sign that leveraged the power of social norms and peer pressure, two very powerful (albeit non-monetary) drivers of the GO signal associated with green behaviors. This sign read "Join Your Fellow Guests in Helping to Save the Environment; 75% of guests participated in the towel-reuse program." Hotel guests exposed to this sign were 25% more likely to reuse towels compared to guests in the control group (who saw no sign) and the guests who saw the other two signs. The results got even better if the sign was tweaked to be more specific to the hotel room (e.g. "Nearly 75% of the guests who stayed here in Room 331 reused their towels").

Using fans versus air conditioners

In a study in San Marcos, California, residents were urged to use fans rather than air conditioners (at least occasionally). The message was delivered via public-service messages that were hung on doorknobs. The reasons people were given, however, were varied. People were randomly exposed to one of four possible reasons: (a) one group was told they could save $54 on their monthly utility bill, (b) a second group was told they could prevent the release of 262lb of greenhouse gases every month, (c) a third group was told it was the socially responsible thing to do, and (d) a fourth group was told that "77% of their neighbors were already using fans instead of air conditioners ... Your community's popular choice!" As you might have guessed by now, the fourth, "everyone else is doing it" message had the maximum impact. It reduced energy usage (per month) by 10%; in comparison, none of the other groups reduced energy usage by more than 3%. In the long term, the impact of the other three messages became even weaker; the fourth message, however, continued to reduce energy usage in those households. Another example of the power of social norms and peer pressure, two very powerful non-monetary drivers of the GO signal for such green behaviors.

Smiley faces for energy-efficient homes

Another well-cited example is the success of Power Reports, a personalized power consumption report that households can subscribe to. These reports, created by the consultancy firm OPower, are packaged with the subscriber's utility bill and provide graphs of the household's power usage. Customers can very easily compare their current usage to their past usage as well as to the usage of their peers. Customers can also see how they rank against the average and the most efficient households in their neighborhood. A key intervention was that households that did exceptionally well received a smiley face on their bill! It turns out that households that received the report demonstrated a sustained drop in their energy usage by an average of 2% compared to households that chose not to get the report. A 2% drop may not seem like much; however, in the domain of utility bills it is a big decrease, especially when scaled across millions of homes. It is even more meaningful if you consider the fact that this drop in energy usage was achieved without any costly rebates, tax credits or expensive mass media campaigns. This too is another example of the power of "concordant" non-monetary interventions—one that leverages the power of social norms and nudges people to keep up with the Joneses—in changing green behaviors.

Watering lawns less

In encouraging local residents to reduce their water usage, the Southwest Florida Water Management District exhorted people to water their lawns less frequently. Through various television commercials they promoted the idea of "skip-a-week" (i.e. water the lawns every other week instead of every week). The best results were obtained when the commercial showed neighbors chatting about their water conservation habits and talking about watering their lawns every other week in the winter. These clever commercials can be viewed on YouTube (http://www.youtube.com/watch?v=P-5Jf3Kaa0Q; http://www.you tube.com/watch?v=gdftnNVC6Gg). After that campaign there was an 18% jump in homes practicing "skip-a-week" irrigation. Showing peers talking about not watering their lawns was a tactic that enhanced the GO signal for the behavior.

GO and STOP signal framework and public policy: summary and caveats about some new policy tools

Public policy decisions rely too heavily on the utility-maximization model. Just as an overreliance on the utility-maximization model of human behavior has led to an unreliable, hit-or-miss pattern of predictions for businesses, an overreliance on the utility-maximization approach has led to many costly mistakes for public policy officials. This approach needs to change. We think that the GO and STOP signal framework, along with the P-T-L (predict–test–learn) approach to research, offers a viable alternative. The examples that we describe in this chapter, and the framework's ability to explain and predict these seemingly hit-or-miss patterns of policy interventions, attests to the viability of the GO and STOP signal framework.

In parting, we would like to leave our readers with two public policy examples as food for thought. Both these public policy areas are ripe for applying the GO and STOP signal framework. One is a classic commons problem and relates to the thorny issue of hosting NIMBY projects. The other is about conditional cash transfers (CCTs), which are all the rage in public policy circles these days.

Agreeing to host NIMBY projects

The acronym NIMBY is short for "not-in-my-backyard" and refers to public welfare projects that are extremely important for the community at large but meet with a lot of resistance from the specific neighborhood that hosts those projects. Examples include transportation improvements (rail lines and airports), power plants, wastewater treatment plants, landfills, prisons, half-way houses and homeless shelters. These projects, albeit beneficial to the community, are often fiercely opposed by the specific neighborhood that is proposed for these so-called "noxious" sites. Hence the refrain "not-in-my-backyard." The traditional approach to dealing with this collective action problem was to tax everyone in the community that benefits from the project and then use the money to subsidize those living in the specific neighborhood that accepts hosting the project. This approach involving monetary incentives has not worked very well. Many communities simply will not accept a NIMBY project. In many cases, providing monetary incentives has actually led to lower acceptance rates of NIMBY projects compared to when no compensation was offered.

Why have monetary incentives not been effective and even backfired in this case? What should be the way forward?

We believe that a GO and STOP signal approach would be very useful here. It is clear that monetary incentives have not only not worked but also backfired. At the same time, however, we would caution against a blind, reactionary rush toward non-monetary incentives. Instead we would advocate a careful analysis of the GO and STOP signal drivers in each NIMBY project. The devil is in the details; not all NIMBY projects are the same. The locus of the resistance might be different depending on which NIMBY project one looks at. Some projects might suffer from very strong STOP signals despite having reasonably strong GO signals as well (e.g. rail lines, airports). Other projects might suffer primarily from very weak GO signals (e.g. prisons, half-way houses). Yet others might suffer primarily from exceptionally strong STOP signals (e.g. landfills, sewage plants). Monetary interventions might work better in the first case (e.g. rail lines, airports) where strong GO signals are already present and the monetary incentive serves to reduce the STOP signal. However, in the latter two cases non-monetary interventions should work better. For example, acceptability of prisons and half-way houses might be low because the GO signals are very weak, as in, people wonder, "How are we better off with prisons?" In this case, a public awareness campaign informing viewers about the larger societal good that such projects bring about might work better. Similarly, acceptability of landfills and sewage treatment plants might be low because of fears of noxious smells, fumes and potential health hazards (even though people understand the importance and societal good related to such projects). Many of these drivers of the STOP signal—noxious smells, fumes and health hazards—are often imaginary fears. In this case, an awareness campaign that assuages these fears will increase the acceptability of the project.

Overall, what is required is a careful analysis of the GO and STOP signal drivers of these NIMBY projects and an attempt to understand where the resistance toward the project is located. Depending on whether the problem lies with a weak GO signal or a strong STOP signal, and whether the key GO or STOP signal driver is social, personal non-monetary, or personal monetary, appropriate "concordant" interventions should be designed. Additionally, an analysis should be conducted to check for potential side effects. Above all, a hedgehogian rush toward either monetary or non-monetary interventions—whichever happens to be the flavor of the day in public policy circles—should be avoided at all cost.

Conditional cash transfers

As a final example, consider the increasing popularity of a new intervention tool that is often referred to as conditional cash transfer (CCT). Such interventions are usually carried out in extremely poor communities, especially if the community tends to neglect critical "human capital" investments such as education and preventative healthcare. In such case, as the moniker suggests, community members (e.g. parents) are given cash incentives that are *conditional* on certain positive behaviors (e.g. their children attending school). Such CCTs have become wildly popular and are used for a variety of purposes, ranging from incentivizing parents to immunize their children and use mosquito nets at home, to incentivizing children to attend school. Abhijit Banerjee and Esther Duflo, two renowned economists from MIT, describe many such CCT programs in their bestselling book *Poor Economics* (2011). In India the government is spending tremendous resources to roll out an ID card scheme with biometric capabilities for its 1 billion citizens, in large part motivated by the ability to administer CCT programs to the rural poor. In short, CCT programs are all the rage in policy circles.

Despite the popular enthusiasm, however, scientific studies assessing the efficacy of CCT programs have revealed mixed results. Some programs succeed in their objectives while many fail. For example, CCT programs seem to have a positive effect on children's school attendance but fail to improve educational outcomes. Similarly they seem to have a positive effect on the intake of medicines but fail to improve overall health outcomes.

What could explain such a hit-or-miss pattern of achievements?

We believe that blindly applying CCT programs, which is essentially a monetary incentive, to all types of "human capital" underinvestment problems has led to this hit-or-miss pattern of success for CCT programs. This is yet another area that will benefit from a careful application of the GO and STOP signal framework and the predict–test–learn approach.

Consider, for example, conflicting findings about school attendance versus educational outcomes, and taking medicines versus health outcomes. Before applying the CCT intervention policy makers should try to understand—what is the root cause of low attendance? Is it the case that the GO signals are very weak? That is, do parents and children simply not understand the value of going to school? Or is it the case that while parents and children understand the value of going to school (i.e. GO signals are reasonably strong), there are other forces that stop them from attending school (e.g. requiring children to help with farm work)? In the former case a monetary incentive such as CCT can easily backfire and we might end up observing the pattern that these scientific studies have revealed. That is, parents send their children to school in an instrumental fashion, simply to earn the cash transfer, but not because of their intrinsic valuation of the benefits of education and learning. This is perhaps why these scientific studies assessing the efficacy of CCT programs observe an improvement on attendance but not on educational and learning outcomes. However, if the latter is the case, then a monetary intervention such as CCT programs should be very effective as it would dampen the monetary STOP signal driver and free up the strong GO signal to have its usual desirable effect.

The same logic applies to the conflicting findings on medicine intake versus health outcomes. It would be important to find out the locus of the problem. Is it the case that the GO signals are too weak? That is, do parents and children simply not understand the benefits of taking medicines, getting immunized and so on? Or is it the case that while the GO signals are strong (i.e. parents understand the benefits), there are also very strong STOP signals that prevail? CCT programs are unlikely to be effective in the former case and might even backfire. CCT programs might be effective in the latter case *if* the STOP signal has a monetary basis (e.g. lacking funds to buy medicines) but not if the STOP signal is non-monetary in nature (e.g. belief in the efficacy of "Western" medicines).

In summary, public policy interventions have suffered from the same kind of hit-or-miss patterns of success that have been observed in the domain of consumer behavior. A careful reconsideration of the classic utility-maximization approach is in order, as the classic approach often leads to interventions that backfire. This is especially true for the domain of public policy as policy makers are typically interested in behaviors that represent a "civic virtue." In such cases, be it recycling, voting or donating blood, human behavior is governed by a delicate balance between internal and external compliance forces. Even well-intentioned policy interventions can easily upset this balance and cause undesirable outcomes. Attempting to strengthen the external compliance forces, for example via monetary sanctions, might disproportionately weaken the internal compliance forces. As a consequence, actual compliance behavior might go down significantly. It seems like our brains are incapable of simultaneously and rationally processing both our internal urge to behave well and public policy admonishments or encouragements to be good citizens.

As Einstein had once famously remarked: "You cannot simultaneously prepare for war and plan for peace." In designing policy interventions it is absolutely paramount to take this handicap into account.

chapter 10

Five steps to actionable consumer insights

How to lead and manage the insights process

So you think you have a bright idea?

The head of innovations at OSRAM Sylvania is leading a new product development project on an LED-based lighting system. The innovation, tentatively called the SmartLite system, promises to be a breakthrough innovation in the lighting market. The company, a global leader in lighting products, has already announced to the world the wonderful things their intelligent lighting system can do:

> Imagine a perfect start to the day. As you start waking up, SmartLite will start automatically simulating the sunrise to fully wake you up. The SmartLite system will also, without any intervention on your part, automatically turn on the coffee machine to start the morning brew. With the smell of fresh coffee in the air, the lighting system informs the window shades to slowly open to synchronize the light with the sunrise. It also turns on the radio to play your favorite wake-up song. SmartLite is the first step toward truly intelligent lighting system. It will know your needs, sense your mood, know your agenda—and automatically provide the right light where you need it, when you need it, even before you know you need it. And to top it all, it will significantly lower your electricity bills.

The managers as OSRAM Sylvania know that their new LED lighting system is better than the traditional lighting system; LED lights offers better-quality lighting at lower operating cost. The managers are certain that the traditional incandescent bulbs soon will be obsolete. Twenty years from now, maybe even sooner, most people will not be using the conventional incandescent bulbs. Yet, the managers at OSRAM Sylvania are also mindful that being a technology pioneer does not guarantee success in the marketplace. Astute positioning and a good go-to-market strategy would be critical for success. And this requires consumer insight. Not just good-to-know con- sumer insight, but actionable consumer insight that can guide product development, branding and distribu- tion decisions. SmartLite's path-breaking features accords it many advan- tages over conventional lighting systems—it is more convenient to use, indeed you don't even have to think about it much as it can be automated; it conserves energy and significantly lowers utility bills; it has productivity- enhancing effects; it improves the quality of light and ergonomics at home, you can having a morning hue or an evening hue; it could provide relief from migraine headaches; and it could be great for social events. Clearly there are a multitude of possibilities. And with great possibilities come many critical choices. Should OSRAM Sylvania focus more on energy savings, on the aesthetic benefits or on health benefits? Should they target consumers who are eager to beautify their homes or those who want to reduce their energy bills? What kind of research should they do, if any?

* * * * * *

In 2013, the government officials at the US Department of Health and Human Services were facing a vexing challenge: how to get the uninsured young adults who view the world through rose-tinted glasses to sign up for health insurance.

The government is committed to providing healthcare coverage for every- one, including the relatively young and the unemployed who don't have coverage from their employers. Despite some opposition, most people agree that this is a good idea. Now, however, economic calculations and actuarial analysis suggests that to meet this objective in a cost-effective manner, it is imperative to get young people on board. But it is not easy to get these young folks to sign up for health insurance because many of them feel they will never need to visit the hospital. How should one go about persuading these young adults, who live with the false sense of security that they will never need medical attention, to sign up for health insurance?

To answer this question, these government officials will need action-able consumer insights. First, they will need insights into why the young adults are not signing up for health insurance. Is it because of weak GO

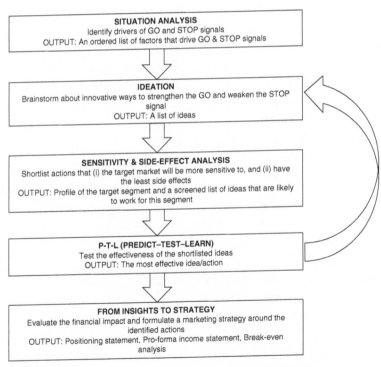

FIGURE 10.1 / Five steps to identify actionable consumer insights

signals ("Insurance is not useful") or is it because of strong STOP signals ("Insurance is useful but I don't want to spend too much time/money on it")? Based on these insights, they will have to address whether they should use traditional or unorthodox messages to sell health insurance. That is, should they use a serious tone and talk about the dire consequences of not having insurance when an unforeseen accident or health hazard occurs? Or should they use advertisements that adopt an unorthodox humor appeal to grab the youngsters' attention?

Five steps to actionable insights

Whether it is selling a new product or formulating a public policy, consumer insights are vital for devising strategies that will work in the marketplace. Consumer insights can help managers to identify what will work and what will not. Thus consumer insights can reduce failure rates and wasteful spending. Despite its promise, we know many managers who do not believe in the power of consumer insights. One of the reasons why managers tend to ignore consumer insights is that many of the so-called consumer insight experts often peddle insights that are not actionable. They conduct surveys and come back with statements such as "58% of the consumers are not happy with their current lighting products," or "63% of the adults under 30 believe that they do not need health insurance." Such statements are good to know. But they seldom spur marketing actions.

The GO-STOP framework can be the basis for generating actionable consumer insights. In this final chapter of the book we outline a step-by-step process that managers can follow to identify actionable consumer insights. We have successfully used this process in classrooms and executive training programs. An outline of the five steps is presented in Figure 10.1. The first three steps can be completed in a short duration—as short as three to ten days—if the required information is readily available. Steps four and five could take several months, depending on the nature of data and analyses required. We describe each of these steps in some detail below.

Step 1: situation analysis

The first step in generating actionable consumer insights entails assessing the GO-STOP status quo. In other words, this step should uncover the existing drivers of the GO and STOP signals that are associated with the product, service or behavior in question. As we discussed in the first two chapters, we believe that the essence of many purchase decisions can be distilled down to two fundamental and often opposing drivers: GO signals that motivate a consumer to approach and buy the product and STOP signals that inhibit him or her from spending money on the product. The GO signal results in an approach tendency and energizes the potential buyers toward the product. It comprises all the thoughts and feelings that attract the potential buyer toward the product or service in question. It is what drives the potential buyer's motivation to consume the product or service. The GO signal, if not inhibited by the STOP signal, will result in

TABLE 10.1 GO-STOP signal activators for SmartLite (output of step 1)

GO Signal Drivers—Reasons to Purchase (respondents who said they will definitely or probably buy)	% of Respondents
This will make it much easier to control the lighting at our home	58%
This will help us realize significant energy cost savings	57%
This will help set a better mood around our home	48%
This will help improve the quality of light at my home	46%
This will improve the aesthetic appeal of my home lighting	45%
This will make my social events more fun	34%
This will improve productivity in work environments	30%
Stop Signal Drivers—Reasons to Not Purchase (respondents who said they might not, probably not, definitely not buy)	**% of Respondents**
Product is too expensive	57%
Product is not good value	13%
Cheaper existing products will work just as well	13%
Product benefits are not credible	9%
Product will not work as expected	6%

Source: Data from Manoj Thomas (2014), Osram Sylvania Case Study, Cornell University.

a purchase. In contrast, the STOP signal results in an avoidance tendency that inhibits action. It comprises all the thoughts and feelings that repel or hold back the potential buyer from the product or service in question.

Note that, as discussed in several chapters of the book, the GO and STOP signals could be driven by subconscious factors; so it might not be easy for managers to identify such latent drivers of GO and STOP signals. Nevertheless, in this first step, managers should try to list all manifest drivers of GO and STOP signals. Managerial intuition, focus group discussions with users and non-users, in-depth interviews and preliminary surveys with concept tests would be appropriate places to start generating the drivers of GO and STOP signals.

Let us illustrate this process with the SmartLite example. To understand the manifest drivers of GO and STOP signals for the new lighting product, we conducted an online survey. Participants in this survey were first shown the new product concept. They were asked to indicate on a five-point scale how likely they are to buy this product. Those who said they will probably or definitely buy the product (around 38% of the respondents said so) were then given a list of reasons and asked to indicate why they said they would buy the product. The results are summarized in the upper panel of Table 10.1. These results give us some idea of the manifest drivers of GO signals for the product.

Those who said that they are unlikely to buy this new product (the remaining 62%) were also asked to indicate the reasons for not purchasing the product. Their responses are summarized in the lower panel of Table 10.1.

Thus, the key output of this session is an ordered list of factors that activate the GO and STOP signals. Table 10.1 provides some insights into the factors that are encouraging the consumers to buy the product as well as those factors that are inhibiting the purchase decision in the current set-up.

At this juncture we would like to elaborate on a cautionary point that we noted in Chapter 2. Recall that we briefly mentioned that consumer self-reports can be unreliable and, therefore, on some occasions, a GO signal might masquerade as a STOP signal (or vice versa). For example, in a consumer's self-reports he or she might list the presence of a discount as a driver of the GO signal, whereas in reality the discount might be weakening the STOP signal (as it usually does). Now, the tricky question for managers here is—is a discount truly a driver of this customer's GO signal, or does it actually weaken the STOP signal? In such cases managers can gain some clarity by asking themselves whether sensitivity to that signal driver would be greater in a benefit-maximization mindset or in a pain-minimization mindset. If the sensitivity to the signal driver is likely to be greater under a benefit-maximization mindset then it is more appropriate to classify the driver as a driver of the GO signal. Conversely, if the sensitivity to the signal driver is likely to be greater under a pain-minimization mindset then it is more appropriate to classify the driver as a driver of the STOP signal. When it comes to a discount, consumers' sensitivity to the presence or absence of discounts is likely to be greater when they are in a pain-minimization mindset than when they are in a benefit-maximization mindset. This is usually (though not always) the case. Thus, it is more appropriate for managers to classify discounts as a driver of the STOP signal, even if a consumer erroneously lists discounts as a driver of their GO signal.

Once the innovation team has a good idea of the drivers of GO and STOP signals, they can then proceed to the second step of the consumer insight-generation process.

Step 2: ideation

This step involves brainstorming about various possible ways of strengthening the GO signals and weakening the STOP signals associated with the product or service. Obviously, the type of brainstorming would vary depending on whether the product being considered is a new product or an existing product. During this brainstorming session, the leader of the innovation group would present two key questions to the group to direct the brainstorming session: what can we do to increase the GO signals for our product? What can we do to weaken the STOP signals for our product? These two questions could be addressed in parallel or in sequence.

This brainstorming activity should involve managers with good knowledge of the product and familiarity with the (potential) consumers of the product. It is important to make sure that the best practices in brainstorming are followed. Ralph Keeney, a professor of decision sciences, argues that in order to facilitate effective brainstorming the following two prerequisites must be met.

First, participants should know the problem to be solved. The leader of the innovation team should define the problem as precisely as possible to the participants much before the brainstorming session. For instance, in the case of the lighting product, the leader should tell the participants that the objective is to develop a positioning strategy for the new lighting product and should circulate the key positioning decisions that need to be taken. In the case of health insurance, participants should be told that the objective is to find out what messaging will encourage young adults to sign up for health insurance.

Second, participants in the brainstorming session should be encouraged to come prepared with their own ideas to share in these sessions. Group brainstorming sessions typically yield good results only if the individuals have thought about the problem *beforehand*, before coming to the session. Keeney argues that brainstorm participants should create a list of alternatives prior to having a group discussion. "Most brainstorming sessions skip this step. Instead, the group comes up with solutions. The danger is that having everyone together during the initial brainstorm can result in a sort of 'group think' instead of individual ideas," says Keeney.

Another important caveat for the ideation stage is to guard against a managerial tendency to be hedgehogian in their brainstorming. That is, managers might inadvertently list only marketing ideas or "solutions" that have worked for them in their past managerial experiences. Participants in the focus groups should be encouraged to overcome this tendency. They should be exhorted to come up with novel and creative ways to strengthen the GO signal and weaken the STOP signal but that are unencumbered by their past experiences.

The output of this second stage would be an exhaustive list of alternatives available to the innovation team. Note that the facilitator or the leader of this brainstorming process should not attempt to screen out ideas at this stage. The objective in the second stage is to creatively generate as many sensible, or at least reasonably sensible, ideas as possible to strengthen the GO signal and/or weaken the STOP signal. Participants, therefore, should be encouraged to think outside the box and unorthodox creative suggestions should be welcomed and documented. The only qualifying constraint for an idea should be that the proposed action should either strengthen the GO signal or weaken the STOP signal. That is, it should be actionable.

Step 3: sensitivity and side-effect analyses

The next step entails screening the ideas. Depending on the number and profile of managers involved, step 3 can be carried out by the same brainstorming group involved in step 2 or by a smaller committee of more empowered managers on the innovation team. This step entails two distinct activities: identifying the most appropriate target market for the product and then screening the options generated in step 2 by considering this target market's needs and motivations.

Let us first consider how to identify the target market. Segmentation is a crucial step in marketing. A common marketing mistake, and some would argue the easiest way to go out of business, is to attempt to be all things to all people. Effective marketing requires segmentation of the market. It is based on the premise that all customers do not have the same needs and wants, yet there are clusters of customers who have similar needs and wants. So a marketer should strive to identify the cluster of consumers who have similar motivations and beliefs, and target all the marketing activities at this segment. Segmentation is usually done through quantitative analysis of benefits that customers seek.[1] Let us illustrate this point with the lighting products case study.

Effective marketing requires segmentation of the market

---

[1] There are other ways of segmenting the market. Some researchers use demographic and psychographic characteristics as segmentation variables, but we recommend benefit segmentation whenever it is feasible.

TABLE 10.2   Market segmentation for SmartLite (to be used as a decision input in step 3)

Reasons to Purchase the New Lighting Product	Cluster 1 (54%)	Cluster 2 (46%)
This will help improve the quality of light at my home	24%	76%
This will improve the aesthetic appeal of my home lighting	37%	57%
This will make my social events more fun	10%	57%
This will help us realize significant energy cost savings	67%	47%
This will help set a better mood around our home	8%	97%
This will make it much easier to control the lighting at our home	61%	54%
This will improve productivity in work environments	20%	45%
Cluster Profile		
Age	38	37
Male	53%	63%
Expected Price	$164	$181
Willing to Pay	$177	$198
Household Size	2.9	3.4
mp3 Player Ownership	53%	62%
Video Game Ownership	59%	69%

Source: Data from Manoj Thomas (2014), Osram Sylvania Case Study, Cornell University.

For the lighting product considered in the opening example, we clustered the prospective buyers (those who said they will buy the product) into two segments based on the benefits they seek.[2] The purchase motivations and profiles of the two segments are summarized in Table 10.2. The upper panel of this table lists how the two segments differ on the benefits sought, while the lower panel reflects how they differ in terms of demographic variables, willingness to pay and purchase habits. Note that only the variables in the upper panel were used for clustering; the variables in the lower cluster enable us to profile each cluster.

---

[2] We used a statistical procedure called k-means clustering.

This analysis reveals the existence of two distinct market segments. The first segment—let us call them energy savers—is motivated to buy the new lighting product in order to save energy. The second segment—the experiencers—is motivated by the improvements in quality of life brought about by this new product. The experiencers are keen to buy this new lighting product because it promises to brighten the mood in their home and improve the quality of light. The latter segment was also willing to pay a higher price for this product and has slightly different demographic profiles and ownership patterns of electronic gadgets.

So, the task at hand for the innovation team is to decide which of the two segments to target. This is a strategic decision with implications for market size and profitability. Therefore, the senior business managers will have to be involved in this decision and they have to sign off on this decision.

After the target market has been identified, the innovation team has to evaluate how the target market will respond to each of the ideas identified in the ideation stage. Specifically, the innovation team should consider the marketing action suggested in each idea generated in step 2 and subject it to the following two screening questions:

(i) Will the target market care about the proposed change?
(ii) Will there be any unintended side effects from the proposed change?

For an idea to pass this screening stage, it should qualify on both these considerations. That is, the target market should be sensitive to the proposed marketing action and there should be no unintended side effect of the proposed action. Such a screening process will cull the viable ideas from the initial list.

Thus, step 3 would produce two distinct outputs. At the completion of step 3, participants would have generated a clear profile of the target customer. Additionally, they would have pruned the list of ideas generated in step 2 to include only those that are likely to resonate well with the identified target segment. A schematic depiction of such a pruned list is shown in Table 10.3.

TABLE 10.3   Market segmentation for SmartLite (output of step 3)

Ideas	Target Market Sensitive	Any Unintended Side Effect?
Idea 1	No	Yes
Idea 2	No	No
Idea 3	No	Yes
Idea 4	Yes	Yes
Idea 5	No	No
Idea 6	Yes	No
Idea 7	Yes	No
Idea 8	Yes	No

Source: Data from Manoj Thomas (2014), Osram Sylvania Case Study, Cornell University.

Step 4: Predict–test–learn (P-T-L)

The next step is testing. Remember what David Ogilvy said about testing: "The most important word in the vocabulary of advertising is test. If you pretest your product with consumers, and pretest your advertising, you will do well in the marketplace." Now that the innovation team has a shortlist of viable recommendations, the next step would be to translate these ideas to testable predictions and then test these predictions. As noted in Chapter 1, testable predictions entail two elements—a proposed change (scientists refer to this as the treatment or the independent variable) and the effect of that change on consumer behavior (scientists refer to this as the outcome or the dependent variable). Testable predictions are often more meaningful when the decision maker has two or more of them based on competing insights. In Chapter 1, we gave examples of two predictions for an orange-juice brand, based on very distinct consumer insights:

Prediction 1: if we reduce our price to attract price-sensitive customers (treatment variable), then our overall sales will improve by 5% (outcome variable).

Prediction 2: if we increase the frequency of consumption of our regular customers by introducing a smaller single-serve pack (treatment variable), then our overall sales will improve by 5% (outcome variable).

The first prediction is based on the assumption that the target market will be more responsive to lower prices. The second prediction is based on the assumption that the target market will be more sensitive to convenient packaging.

An important decision in this stage is about the nature of the test—should it be a market test, a product test or simply an online concept test? Market tests can be done in select retail stores or select geographies. Market tests are the most reliable form of test. However, they also tend to be very expensive and require manufacturing as well as distribution capabilities.[3] Therefore, innovation teams often have to make do with the less expensive and easier-to-administer product tests and concept tests.

If the focus is on product usage experience, then product usage tests would be most appropriate; different groups of consumers could be given different versions of the product and their responses could be compared with the control group. Product usage tests would be appropriate, for example, if the marketer is testing a new 3D TV or a new type of food product. In software development parlance, such a test would be referred to as a beta test in which a sample of the intended audience tries out the product.

However, if the innovation team's objective is to test the effect of an idea—a positioning message or a new benefit—then concept tests would suffice. If the message is on a webpage or an online application, then A/B testing would be the best way to go. In fact, even for physical products, if the objective is to test positioning or messaging ideas, online concept tests that are similar to A/B tests would suffice. Randomly selected groups of participants could be shown different versions of the concept and the innovation team could compare the purchase intentions of different groups.

For instance, if the innovation team working on the lighting product wants to test the three shortlisted ideas from step 3, they could create three different concept statements, each implementing one idea, and

---

[3] Sometimes the cost of market research could be higher than the expected value of a product launch without research. In such cases, it might make more sense to implement the proposed change without doing additional research.

present each idea to one of three randomly selected groups of participants. No group would see more than one idea. Thus, this would be an experiment with three conditions (the technical name of such a test is between-participants experiment). Such a test is much more reliable than presenting all three concepts in a focus group and asking them which concept they prefer. Using such an experiment, the innovation team can not only test whether purchase intentions vary across the three groups, but they can also test whether the reasons to buy (GO signals) and the reasons not to buy (STOP signals) vary across the three treatment conditions. Thus, such a test would help them to decide which of the three ideas is most promising.

One aspect needs to be highlighted: the most important variable in such a test is actual purchase or purchase intention. Therefore, if it is a product test or a concept test, this purchase question should be administered first. The process measures—the reasons to buy (GO signals) and the reasons not to buy (STOP signals)—should come only after the participants share the purchase decisions. As noted in Chapter 1, it is always good practice to collect and analyze some additional "segmentation"-related data (e.g. age, gender, income, socioeconomic status or other individual-level variables) because sometimes the analysis might reveal that the intervention is more effective among certain subgroups of the sample (e.g. families with kids versus families without kids).

Finally, it is important for the prediction team to brace themselves for failures. Not all predictions will pan out. In fact, the chances are that most predictions will not pan out. Predicting human behavior is not an easy business. Keep in mind that there is learning even if the predictions "fail" as it probably indicates that the key intervention is not effective, thus freeing up managers to pursue other more efficacious interventions. As Jeff Bezos said: "Invention requires experimentation and experimentation implies failure. If you know it's going to work, then it's not an experiment." If the predictions fail, then the innovation team should consider what they have learned about consumer behaviors from the testing, and then go back to the ideation stage to generate new predictions. The iterative cycle should continue till they come up with interventions that change consumer behaviors.

Thus, the final output from this stage is identification of the most promising idea. What started as an idea in step 2 would have by the end of step 4 become a validated consumer insight.

Step 5: from insights to strategy

The next step is to translate this consumer insight into a business plan. The specific activities in this step would vary depending on the marketing action that is being considered. If the proposed marketing action entails a significant capital investment, then a break-even analysis would be required. Such a break-even analysis would require reliable estimates of the capital outlay, separate estimates of cannibalized and incremental sales, the proposed price and contribution margins. Furthermore, if the project has a significant impact on the capital outlay of the organization, then a pro-forma profit and loss statement would also be in order. The excellent book on strategic marketing by Roger Kerin and Robert Peterson (*Strategic Marketing Problems: Cases and Comments*, 2012) offers a good overview of these financial analyses. As is clear from this discussion, this step would require the active participation of managers from the finance department.

If the consumer insight is being used to position a new product or reposition an existing product, then a positioning statement would be in order. A positioning statement is the fountainhead of most marketing decisions. It succinctly articulates the demographic and psychographic attributes of the target market, the category in which the new product would be competing (often referred to as the frame of reference, because the target market compares the new product with products in this category), and the differentiating features that strengthen the GO signal or weaken the STOP signal. Some positioning statements also have an additional statement explaining why the target market would find the claims about differentiation credible. A typical positioning statement would have the format shown in Table 10.4.

TABLE 10.4 **Format of a positioning statement (output of step 5)**

To _____ (target market defined in terms of the benefits they seek), the _____ (new product or brand) is a _____ (frame of reference or category) that _____ (differentiating features that strengthens the GO signal or weakens the STOP signal or both) because _____ (reason to believe the differentiating claim).

As an example, recall Nabisco's 100-calorie-pack innovation that was discussed in Chapter 2. Given all that we know about what contributed to its success, the positioning statement for the 100-calorie cookie pack would read as follows: "To health-conscious consumers who are concerned about their calorie intake, the Keebler's 100-calorie pack is a brand of chocolate chip cookies that prevents overconsumption of calories without compromising on taste, because the cookies are packed in 100-calorie serving portions."

If the innovation is an advertising message or design work, then a draft creative brief could be an output of the exercise. A creative brief is a document that reflects the agreement between a client and designer before any work begins. Throughout the design project, the creative brief continues to inform and guide the work. A good creative brief will specify the target market, the intended outcome and the constraints.

In summary, the five steps identified in this chapter can guide the identification of actionable consumer insights. Consumer insights are not necessarily an act of serendipity. Jennifer Mueller, a creativity researcher at the University of San Diego points out: "The stereotype is that creativity just has to be unleashed, and it's not true. It has to be tightly managed. You have to know how to foster it." The five steps outlined in this chapter are a predictable and actionable blueprint for generating and managing consumer insights. Following the five steps, managers can identify innovative drivers of GO and STOP signals, test whether those drivers will work as intended and then use those insights to guide their strategic decisions.

Glossary

Actionable consumer insight: an actionable consumer insight is a prediction about how a change in any marketing mix element will influence consumer behavior.

Affective and cognitive decisions: judgments and decisions can be based on affective responses (hot processes) or based on purely cognitive evaluations (cold processes). Both GO and STOP signals can vary on the extent to which they are based on hot versus cold processes. This leads to a typology of four different types of purchase decisions, as summarized in Table G.1.

Discordant pricing: if a brand's price is discordant with consumers' mindset, then it will reduce their willingness to buy the brand. When purchase intentions are more sensitive to functional, social or psychological benefits of the product (benefit-maximization mindset), lower prices can be seen as discordant and can reduce sales. When purchase intentions are more sensitive to the pain of paying

TABLE G.1 Four different types of purchase decisions

	cold STOP signal	hot STOP signal
hot GO signal	purchase decision influenced by strong desire	conflict between strong desire and guilt/regret
cold GO signal	dispassionate evaluation of pros and cons	purchase decision influenced by guilt/regret

(pain-minimization mindset), higher prices can be seen as discordant and can reduce sales.

GO signal: a GO signal is a thought, feeling or a subconscious response that creates an approach tendency and energizes the potential buyers toward the product. It is what drives the potential buyer's motivation to consume the product or service. The GO signal, if not inhibited by the STOP signal, will result in a purchase. Most obviously, the quality of the product or the key differentiating product attributes can trigger and strengthen the GO signal. However, it is important to note that several other less obvious aspects of the purchase or consumption process could also drive the GO signal. For example, design, packaging and brand name could trigger GO signals. Other aspects of the consumption journey such as the in-store experience, interactions with salespeople, after sales service, social signaling value (i.e. how highly one is perceived by others on being seen using the product) and self-signaling value (i.e. how highly one is perceived in one's own eyes on using the product), to name a few, can also serve as important triggers of the GO signal.

Heuristics: heuristics are simple, efficient rules that enable us to make quick decisions. Heuristics can be learned through prior experience or acquired through evolutionary processes. Heuristic decision making is fast and frugal and is often based on the evaluation of one or two salient bits of information. We use heuristics, sometimes consciously and sometimes unconsciously, to navigate efficiently through the complex maze of everyday decisions. Nobel laureate Daniel Kahneman in his book *Thinking Fast and Slow* defines a heuristic as a "simple procedure that helps find adequate, though often imperfect, answers to difficult questions." Gerd Gigerenzer and Wolfgang Gaissmaier of the Max Planck Institute of Human Development, Berlin, offer the following definition of a heuristic: "A heuristic is a strategy that ignores part of the information, with the goal of making decisions more quickly, frugally, and/or accurately than complex methods."

Mindset: a mindset refers to a mental inclination, tendency or habit that makes people predisposed to engage in certain type of cognitive processing. Benefit-maximization and pain-minimization mindsets could be considered two ends of a continuum of mindsets that differ in the relative sensitivity to GO signals and STOP signals. The benefit-maximization mindset makes people more sensitive to functional, social or psychological benefits of the product. People in a pain-minimization mindset are more sensitive to the reduction in the aversive feelings or thoughts caused by parting with money, regret or risk.

P-T-L: an acronym for the predict–test–learn approach to market research. This approach to market research follows the hypothesis-testing format followed in scientific research. The investigator (i.e. the manager who is leading the innovation process) first generates a series of testable predictions with clearly specified independent variables and dependent variables. Then these predictions are tested through experiments that are free of other confounding factors. The results of the test are used to learn about drivers of GO and STOP signals. Traditional market research techniques such as focus groups and consumer interviews are useful only to the extent that they can help to generate predictions that can be tested.

Signal driver or trigger: drivers or triggers are factors that activate or strengthen a GO signal or a STOP signal. These could be external factors such as brand name or packaging, or internal factors such as a mental budget or a diet control goal.

STOP signal: a STOP signal is a thought, feeling or a subconscious response that creates an avoidance tendency that inhibits consideration or purchase. It comprises all the signals that repel or hold back the potential buyer from the product or service in question. A STOP signal can manifest in several forms—the pain of paying, anticipated regret, perceived risk, the feeling of uncertainty—all of which can counteract the urge to buy. STOP signals can override the GO signal and prevent potential buyers from buying the product. The most obvious driver of the STOP signal is the price of the product. However, less obvious aspects of the consumption experience can act as brakes and keep the consumer away from the product. For example, the feeling of guilt ("It looks delicious but I feel guilty eating a cookie!") and justifiability ("I cannot justify paying that much for a pencil!"), concerns about the in-store experience ("Too cluttered!"), unpleasant interactions with salespeople ("Too pushy!"), after sales service ("Too little!"), social signaling value ("Does it signal low status to others?") and self-signaling value ("Does it contradict what kind of a person I see myself as?"), to name a few, could easily act as drivers of the STOP signal.

Top-down processing: a judgment is said to be based on top-down information processing when the perceptual and cognitive processes underlying the judgment are influenced by schematic knowledge and a priori expectations. Expectations created by schematic knowledge and product cues can influence the manner in which consumers categorize stimuli and make inferences about latent attributes of the stimuli. Top-down processing plays an important role in price–quality inferences. Top-down and bottom-up can be considered as two ends of a continuum of processing modes that differ in the influence of schematic knowledge.

Unconscious, nonconscious or subsconscious processing: an unconscious or a subconscious mental process is one that the person is not aware of. For example, the human mind can rely on heuristic strategies to make a judgment even when the person is not aware of the ongoing mental process. In a similar vein, a person can rely on implicit memory to make judgments even when the person cannot consciously recall the information.

References

Chapter 1

Gilovich, Thomas (1991), *How We Know What Isn't So: The Fallibility of Human Reason in Everyday Life*, Simon & Schuster.

McFadden, Daniel (2014), The New Science of Pleasure, NBER Working Paper No. 18687.

Thomas, Manoj (2013), Commentary on Behavioral Price Research: The Role of Subjective Experiences in Price Cognition, *Academy of Marketing Science Review*, 3 (1), 141–5.

Bentham, Jeremy (1823), *Introduction to Principles and Morals of Legislation*, Dover Publications.

Keller, Kevin Lane (2002), *Branding and Brand Equity*, MSI Relevant Knowledge Series, Marketing Science Institute.

Keller, Kevin Lane (2012), Economic and Behavioral Perspectives on Brand Extension, *Marketing Science*, 31 (September–October), 772–5.

Hoeffler, Steven and Keller, Kevin Lane (2003), The Marketing Advantages of Strong Brands, *Journal of Brand Management*, 10 (August), 421–45.

Alter, Adam (2013), *Drunk Tank Pink: And Other Unexpected Forces that Shape How We Think, Feel, and Behave*, The Penguin Press.

Alter, Adam. L. and Oppenheimer, D. M. (2006), Predicting Short-Term Stock Fluctuations by Using Processing Fluency, *Proceedings of the National Academy of Sciences*, 103, 9369–72.

Frank, Robert H. (2011), The Strategic Role of the Emotions, *Emotion Review*, 3.3, 252–4.

Frank, Robert H. (2007), *The Economic Naturalist: In Search of Explanations for Everyday Enigmas*, Westview Press.

Tetlock, Philip (2006), *Expert Political Judgment: How Good Is It? How Can We Know?*, Princeton University Press.

Winfield, Nick (2013), Tech Companies Press for a Better Retail Experience, *New York Times*, 15 December.

Brody, Jane (2012), Popular Antibiotics May Carry Serious Side Effects, *New York Times*, 10 September.

Isaacson, Walter (2011), *Steve Jobs*, Simon & Schuster.

Beahm, George (2011), *I, Steve: Steve Jobs in His Own Words*, Hardie Grant Publishing.

Guadagni, Peter and Little, John D. C. (1983), A Logit Model of Brand Choice Calibrated on Scanner Data, *Marketing Science*, 2 (Summer), 203–8.

Nisbett, Richard and Wilson, Timothy D. (1977), Telling More than We Can Know: Verbal Reports on Mental Processes, *Psychological Review*, 84, 231–59.

Ariely, Dan (2010), Why Businesses Don't Experiment, *Harvard Business Review*, 1 April.

Anderson, Eric T. and Simester, Duncan (2011), A Step-by-Step Guide to Smart Business Experiments, *Harvard Business Review*, 1 March.

Chapter 2

Thompson, Stephanie (2006), Consumers Pay More for Less with 100 Calories Packs, *Advertising Age*, April 2006.

Centre for Science in the Public Interest report on 100 calories prices, 7 July 2007, available at http://cspinet.org/new/200708141.html, date accessed 2 November 2014.

Peters, Jeremy (2007), In Small Packages, Fewer Calories and More Profit, *New York Times*, July 7.

Lewin, Kurt (1943), Defining the Field at a Given Time, *Psychological Review*, 50, 292–310.

Elliot, Andrew (2008), *The Handbook of Approach and Avoidance Motivation*, Psychology Press.

Bentham, Jeremy (1823), *Introduction to Principles and Morals of Legislation*, Dover Publications.

Gray, J. A. (1990), Brain Systems that Mediate both Emotion and Cognition, *Cognition and Emotion*, 4, 269–88.

Carver, C. S. and White, T. L. (1994), Behavioral Inhibition, Behavioral Activation, and Affective Responses to Impending Reward and Punishment: The BIS/BAS Scales, *Journal of Personality and Social Psychology*, 67, 319–33.

Higgins, E. T. (2005), Value from Regulatory Fit. *Current Directions in Psychological Science*, 14, 209–13.

Higgins, E. T. (2000), Making a good decision: Value from fit, *American Psychologist*, 55, 1217–30.

Dougherty, D. M., Mathias, C. W., Marsh, D. M. and Jagar, A. A. (2005), Laboratory Measures of Impulsivity, *Behavior Research Methods*, 37, 82–90.

Harris, M., Penfold, R. B., Hawkins, A., Maccombs, J., Wallace, B. and Reynolds, B. (2014), Dimensions of Impulsive Behavior and Treatment Outcomes for Adolescent Smokers, *Experimental and Clinical Psychopharmacology*, 22, 57–64.

Kahneman, Daniel (2011), *Thinking Fast and Slow*, Farrar, Straus and Giroux.

Gigerenzer, Gerd and Gaissmaier, Wolfgang (2011), Heuristic Decision Making, *Annual Review of Psychology*, Vol. 62 (January), 451–82.

Scott, Maura L., Nowlis, Stephen M., Mandel, Naomi and Morales, Andrea C. (2008), Do 100-Calorie Packs Lead to Increased Consumption? The Effect of Reduced Food Sizes and Packages on the Consumption Behavior of Restrained Eaters and Unrestrained Eaters, *Journal of Consumer Research*, 35 (October), 391–405.

Chandon, Pierre and Wansink, Brian (2012), Does Food Marketing Need to Make Us Fat? A Review and Solutions, *Nutrition Reviews*, 70:10, 571–93.

Wansink, Brian, Payne, Collin R. and Shimizu, Mitsuru (2011), The 100-Calorie Semi-Solution: Sub-Packaging Most Reduces Intake Among the Heaviest, *Obesity*, 19:5 (Spring), 1098–1100.

Wansink, Brian and Chandon, Pierre (2006), Can "Low Fat" Nutrition Labels Lead to Obesity?, *Journal of Marketing Research*, 43 (November), 605–17.

Wansink, Brian (2012), Package Size, Portion Size, Serving Size . . . Market Size: The Unconventional Case for Half-Size Servings, *Marketing Science*, 31:1, 54–7.

Chapter 3

Reingold, Jennifer (2012), Retail's New Radical, *Fortune*, March 19, Vol. 165, Issue 4, 124–31.

Pasquarelli, Adrianne (2012), J.C. Penney Takes Aim at Macy's, *Crain's New York Business*, March 5, Vol. 28, Issue 10, 0001-0001.

Ritson, Mark (2013), The Vital Error at the Core of Penney's Revival, *Marketing Week* (Online Edn), 10 April, 1-1.

Moin, David (2012), Newsmaker of the Year: Ron Johnson, *WWD: Women's Wear Daily*, 10 December, Vol. 204, Issue 119, 2b–1.

Tuttle, Brad (2012), Maybe Shoppers Don't Want "Fair and Square" Prices After All, *Time*, 29 March.

URL for JC Penney's Fair and Square TV ad: https://www.youtube.com/watch?v=K_78iVigjSI, date accessed 2 November 2014.

Brady, Diane (2012), Ron Johnson on the Progress of His JC Penney Remake, *Bloomberg Businessweek*, 9 August.

Ellwood, Mark, *Bargain Fever: Our Obsession with Getting More for Less*, Portfolio/Penguin.

Anderson, Eric T. and Simester, Duncan (2003), Effects of $9 Price Endings on Retail Sales: Evidence from Field Experiments, *Quantitative Marketing and Economics*, 1 (1), 93–110.

Anderson, Eric T. and Simester, Duncan (1998), The Role of Sale Signs, *Marketing Science*, 17 (2), 139–55.

Anderson, Eric T. and Simester, Duncan (2003), Mind Your Pricing Cues, *Harvard Business Review*, 81 (9), 96–103.

Anderson, Eric T. and Simester, Duncan (2001), Are Sale Signs Less Effective When More Products Have Them?, *Marketing Science*, 20 (2), 121–42.

Knutson, B., Rick, S., Wimmer, G. E., Prelec, D. and Loewenstein, G. (2007), Neural Predictors of Purchases, *Neuron*, 53, 147–57.

Tierney, John (2007), The Voices in My Head Say "Buy It!" Why Argue?, *New York Times*, 16 January.

Thomas, Manoj and Morwitz, Vicki G. (2005), Penny Wise and Pound Foolish: The Left Digit Effect in Price Cognition, *Journal of Consumer Research*, 32 (1), 54–65.

Thomas, Manoj and Morwitz, Vicki G. (2009), Heuristics in Numerical Cognition: Implications for Pricing, in Vithala Rao (ed.), *Handbook of Research in Pricing*, Edward Elgar Publishing, pp. 132–49.

Lacetera, Nicola, Pope, Devin G. and Sydnor, Justin R. (2011), Heuristic Thinking and Limited Attention in the Car Market, *American Economic Review*, 102 (5), 2206–36.

Bhattacharya, Utpal, Holden, Craig W. and Jacobsen, Stacey (2012), Penny Wise, Dollar Foolish: Buy-Sell Imbalances On and Around Round Numbers, *Management Science*, 58, 413–31.

Stiving, Mark and Winer, Russell S. (1997), An Empirical Analysis of Price Endings with Scanner Data, *Journal of Consumer Research*, 24 (1), 57–68.

Schindler, Robert M. and Kirby, Patrick N. (1997), Patterns of Rightmost Digits Used in Advertised Prices: Implications for Nine-Ending Effects, *Journal of Consumer Research*, 24 (2), 192–202.

Chapter 4

Robyn, Meredith (2007), The Next People Car, *Forbes*, posted on Yahoo! Finance, 19 April.

Attewill, Fred (2008), World's Cheapest Car Upsets Environmentalists, *Guardian*, 10 January.

Bajaj, Vikas (2010), Tata's Nano, the Car That Few Want to Buy, *New York Times*, 9 January.

Philip, Siddharth (2013), Tata Signals Pricier Nano rafter "Cheapest Car" Tag Flops, Bloomberg, date accessed 11 April 2013.

Press Trust of India (2013), May Launch Nano in Indonesia and Bring Back to India: Ratan Tata, *Economic Times*, 29 November.

Tybout, Alice M. (2011), Positioning the Tata Nano (A), Kellogg Case KEL602.

Shiv, Baba, Carmon, Ziv and Ariely, Dan (2005), Placebo Effects of Marketing Actions: Consumer May Get What they Pay For, *Journal of Marketing Research*, 42 (November), 383–93.

Chapter 5

Welch, David and Kiley, David (2004), Can Caddy's Driver Make GM Cool?, *BusinessWeek*, 20 September, Issue 3900, 105–6.

LaReau, Jamie (2005), A Shot of Inspiration, *Automotive News*, 11 July, Vol. 79, Issue 6158, 8–49.

Chon, Gina (2006), GM Official Regrets Employee Discounting, *Wall Street Journal*, 5 January.

Carty, Sharon Silke (2005), Car Sales Suffer from Employee Discount Program Hangover, *USA Today*, 2 November.

Woodhill, Louis (2012), General Motors Is Headed For Bankruptcy–Again, *Forbes*, 15 August.

Welch, David (2004), GM: A Dangerous Skid, *BusinessWeek*, 1 November, Issue 3906, 40–1.

Flint, Jerry (2002), Money Isn't Everything, *Forbes*, 12 August, Vol. 170, Issue 3, 80–80.

The Economist Intelligence Unit (2010), *Industry Report: Automotive*, September.

Chatterjee, Anjan, Jauchius, Matthew E., Kaas, Hans-Werner and Satpathy, Aurobind (2002), Revving Up Auto Branding, *McKinsey Quarterly*, No. 1, 134–43.

Carty, Sharon Silke (2005), GM Posts $318M Losses Despite Blockbuster Sales, *USA Today*, 2 November.

Stoffer, Harry (2005), GM May Extend Discounts, *Automotive News*, 27 June, Vol. 79, Issue 6154, 1–1.

Boudette, Neal E. (2006), Has GM Finally Hit the Brakes on Sales Slide, *Wall Street Journal* (Eastern edn), 18 July, Vol. 248, Issue 14, B1–B2.

Stein, Jason (2004), GM Marketing Boss: Incentives are Here to Stay, *Automotive News*, 23 August, Vol. 78, Issue 6108, 8–8.

Truett, Richard (2008), GM Repeats Employee Discount Program, *Automotive News*, 4 August, Vol. 82, Issue 6319, 3–3.

Stoll, John D. (2008), Eight-Brand Pileup Dents GM's Turnaround Efforts, *Wall Street Journal*, 4 March, B1–B1.

Robyn, Meredith (2000), Trouble in Paradise, *Forbes*, November 13, Vol. 166, Issue 13, 101–8.

Datamonitor (2006), MarketWatch: Global Round-up, Industry Comment, 12–13 January.

Plassmann, Hilke, O'Doherty, John P., Shiv, Baba and Rangel, Antonio (2008), Marketing Actions Modulate the Neural Representation of Experienced Pleasantness, *Proceedings of the National Academy of Science of the United States of America* (PNAS), Vol. 105, No. 3, January.

Chapter 6

Thomas, Manoj, Morwitz, Vicki and Lodish, Leonard (2009), When Does Expensive Food Taste Better? Top-Down and Bottom-Up Processing in Price-Quality Inferences, Cornell University Working Paper.

Zagat Survey (2002), Zagat 2002 Survey for New York City Restaurants, Zagat Survey, LLC.

Selfridge, O. Gordon (1959), Pandemonium: A Paradigm for Learning, in *Symposium on the Mechanization of Thought Process*, HM Stationery Office, 513–26.

Asch, Solomon E. (1946), Forming Impressions of Personality, *Journal of Abnormal and Social Psychology*, 41, 258–90.

Asch, Solomon E. (1952), *Social Psychology*, Prentice Hall.

Meyers-Levy, Joan and Tybout, Alice (1989), Schema Congruity as a Basis of Product Evaluation, *Journal of Consumer Research*, 12 (June), 31–46.

Meyer, Robert J. (1987), The Learning of Multiattribute Judgment Policies, *Journal of Consumer Research*, 14, 155–73.

Rumelhart, David E. (1989), The Architecture of Mind: A Connectionist Approach, in Michael Posner (ed.), *Foundations of Cognitive Science*, MIT Press, pp. 133–59.

Rao, Akshay R. and Monroe, Kent B. (1989), The Effect of Price, Brand Name, and Store Name on Buyers' Perceptions of Product Quality: An Integrative Review, *Journal of Marketing Research*, 3 (August), 351–7.

Rao, Akshay and Monroe, Kent B. (1988), The Moderating Effect of Prior Knowledge on Cue Utilization in Product Evaluations, *Journal of Consumer Research*, 15 (September), 253–64.

Rao, Akshay R. (2005), The Quality of Price as a Quality Cue, *Journal of Marketing Research*, 42 (November), 401–5.

Monroe, Kent B. (1973), Buyers Subjective Perceptions of Price, *Journal of Marketing Research*, 10 (February), 70–80.

Wathieu, Luc and Bertini, Marco (2007), Price as a Stimulus to Think: The Case for Willful Overpricing, *Marketing Science*, 26 (1), 118–29.

Chartrand, T. L., Huber, J., Shiv, B. and Tanner, R. (2008), Nonconscious Goals and Consumer Choice, *Journal of Consumer Research*, 35, 189–201.

Argo, Jennifer J., Dahl, Darren W. and Manchanda, Rajesh V. (2005), The Influence of a Mere Social Presence in a Retail Context, *Journal of Consumer Research*, 32 (September), 207–12.

Kardes, Frank R., Cronley, Maria L., Kellaris, James J. and Posavac, Steven S. (2004), The Role of Selective Information Processing in Price-quality Inference, *Journal of Consumer Research*, 31 (2), 368–74.

Chapter 7

Farago, R. (2010), Dynamic Pricing Leaves Some Consumers Spending More Than Others, http://www.zippycart.com/ecommerce-news/1185-dynamic-pricing-leaves-consumers-spending-more/, date accessed 2 November 2014.

Streitfeld, D. (2000), On the Web, Price Tags Blur, *Washington Post*, 27 September, A01.

Anderson, Eric T. and Simester, Duncan I. (2008), Does Demand Fall When Customers Perceive That Prices Are Unfair? The Case of Premium Pricing for Large Sizes, *Marketing Science*, Vol. 27, No. 3, May–June, 492–500.

Gourville, John T. (1999), Note on Behavioral Pricing, Harvard Business School, 9-599-114, 25 May.

Heat Playoff History 1997, http://www.nba.com/heat/history/playoff_history_1997.html, date accessed 2 November 2014.

Moore, Stephen (2006), Time for Action On Huggable, Lovable Dolls, *Wall Street Journal*, 24 November.

Richtel, Matt (2007), A Year Later, the Same Scene: Long Lines for the Elusive Wii, *New York Times*, 14 December.

Stoller, G. (2008), Fees Rising for Extra Checked Bags and Overweight Luggage, *USA Today*, 19 February.

Consumer Reports Magazine (2011), Carriers Continue to Squeeze With Fees, http://www.consumerreports.org/cro/magazinearchive/2011/june/money/airlines/airline-fees/index.htm, date accessed 2 November 2014.

Maynard, M. (2008), The Catch Phrase is "A La Carte" as Airlines Push Additional Fees, *New York Times*, 19 June.

Graham, J., Haidt, J. and Nosek, B. A. (2009), Liberals and Conservatives Rely on Different Sets of Moral Foundations, *Journal of Personality and Social Psychology*, 96, 1029–46.

Reinartz, Werner and Kumar, V. (2002), The Mismanagement of Customer Loyalty, *Harvard Business Review*, Product No. 1407.

Hilsenrath, Jon E. and Sanders, Peter (2005), Inflation Toehold? Firms Gain Power to Boost Prices, *New York Times*, 2 November.

Chase, Marilyn (2007), Blind Ambition: Genentech's Big Drug for Eyes Faces a Rival, *Wall Street Journal*, 22 February.

Whoriskey, Peter and Keating, Dan (2013), An Effective Eye Drug is Available for $50 But Many Doctors Choose a $2,000 Alternative, *Washington Post*, 7 December.

Bolton, L. E., Warlop, L. and Alba, J. W. (2003), Consumer Perceptions of Price (Un)Fairness, *Journal of Consumer Research*, 29 (4), 474–91.

Williams, Daniel R., Vogt, Christine A. and Vittersø, Joar (1999), Structural Equation Modeling of User's Responses to Wilderness Recreation Fees, *Journal of Leisure Research*, Vol. 31, No. 3, 245–68.

Kotler, Philip and Waldemar, Pförtsch (2010), *Ingredient Branding – Making the Invisible Visible*, Springer.

Hays, C. L. (1999), Variable-Price Coke Machine Being Tested, *New York Times*, 28 October.

Leonhardt, D. (2005), Why Variable Pricing Fails at the Vending Machine, *New York Times*, 27 June.

Angwin, Julia and Mattioli, Dana (2012), Coming Soon: Toilet Paper Priced Like Airline Tickets, *Wall Street Journal*, 5 September, http://online.wsj.com/articles/SB10000872396390444914904577617333130724846, date accessed 2 November 2014.

Federal Trade Commission (2006), Investigation of Gasoline Price Manipulation and Post-Katrina Gasoline Price Increases, Report, Spring, http://www.ftc.gov/reports/federal-trade-commission-investigation-gasoline-pricemanipulation-post-katrina-gasoline, date accessed 2 November 2014.

Welborn, A. A. and Flynn, A. M. (2005), Price Increases In the Aftermath of Hurricane Katrina: Authority to Limit Price Gouging, CRS Report for Congress, #RS22236 (2 September), http://fas.org/sgp/crs/misc/RS22236.pdf, date accessed 2 November 2014.

scnow.com (2009), SC AG Ends Investigation Over Gas Price Gouging, 9 July, http://www.scnow.com/news/state/article_70496394-de0f-5195-9c39-f227a3390ec6.html, date accessed 2 November 2014.

State of South Carolina Office of the Attorney General (2009), Gas Price Gouging Report, 25 June, http://www.scattorneygeneral.com/newsroom/pdf/2009/gaspricegouging.pdf, date accessed 2 November 2014.

Badertscher, N. (2005), 15 Cited for Gouging Gas Prices, *Atlanta Journal-Constitution*, November 16, Home Edn, 1B.

Chapter 8

Durkin, Thomas A. (2000), Credit Cards: Use and Consumer Attitudes, *Federal Reserve Bulletin*, September.

Humphrey, David B. (2004), Replacement of Cash by Cards in U.S. Consumer Payments, *Journal of Economics and Business Research*, 56 (4), 211–25.

Nilson Report (2007), The Nilson Report, trade publication on consumer payment systems, Issue 890, October.

Center for Disease Control and Prevention website at http://www.cdc.gov/obesity/data/adult.html, date accessed 2 November 2014.

Ogden, Cynthia L., Carroll, Margaret D., Curtin, Lester R., McDowell, Margaret A., Tabak, Carolyn J. and Flegal, Katherine M. (2006), Prevalence of Overweight and Obesity in the United States, 1999–2004, *Journal of the American Medical Association*, 295 (13), 1549–55.

Prelec, Drazen and Loewenstein, George (1998), The Red and the Black: Mental Accounting of Savings and Debt, *Marketing Science*, 17 (1), 4–28.

Soman, Dilip (2001), Effects of Payment Mechanism on Spending Behavior: The Role of Rehearsal and Immediacy of Payments, *Journal of Consumer Research*, 27 (4), 460–74.

Soman, Dilip and Cheema, Amar (2002), The Effect of Credit on Spending Decisions: The Effect of Credit Limit and Credibility, *Marketing Science*, 21 (1), 32–53.

Raghubir, Priya and Srivastava, Joydeep (2008), Monopoly Money: The Effect of Payment Coupling and Form on Spending Behavior, *Journal of Experimental Psychology: Applied*, 14 (3), 213–25.

Raghubir, Priya and Srivastava, Joydeep (2009), The Denomination Effect, *Journal of Consumer Research*, 36 (4), 701–13.

Feinberg, Richard A. (1986), Credit Cards as Spending Facilitating Stimuli: A Conditioning Interpretation, *Journal of Consumer Research*, 13 (3), 348–56.

McCall, Michael and Belmont, Heather J. (1996), Credit Card Insignia and Restaurant Tipping: Evidence for an Associative Link, *Journal of Applied Psychology*, Vol. 81 (5), 609–13.

Thomas, Manoj (2013), Commentary on Behavioral Price Research: The Role of Subjective Experiences in Price Cognition, *Academy of Marketing Science Review*, 3 (1), 141–5.

Thomas, Manoj, Desai, Kalpesh and Seenivasan, Satheeshkumar (2011), How Credit Card Payments Increase Unhealthy Food Purchases: Visceral Regulation of Vices, *Journal of Consumer Research*, 38 (1), 126–39.

Wertenbroch, Klaus (1998), Consumption Self-Control by Rationing Purchase Quantities of Virtue and Vice, *Marketing Science*, 17 (4), 1–10.

Rick, Scott I., Cryder, Cynthia E. and Loewenstein, George (2008), Tightwads and Spendthrifts, *Journal of Consumer Research*, 34 (April), 767–82.

Rook, Dennis (1987), The Buying Impulse, *Journal of Consumer Research*, 14 (September), 189–99.

Ubel, Peter A. (2009), *Free Market Madness*, Harvard Business Press.

Wansink, Brian (2006), *Mindless Eating – Why We Eat More Than We Think*, Bantam-Dell.

Lieber, Ron (2014), The Most Serious Threat When Using Credit Cards: You, *New York Times*, 10 October.

Toffler, Alvin (1984), *The Future Shock*, Bantam.

Chapter 9

Titmuss, R. M. (1970), *The Gift Relationship*, Allen & Unwin.

Titmuss, R. M. (1971), The Gift of Blood, Trans-action, VIII, now in R. M. Titmuss, B. Abel-Smith and K. Titmuss (eds) (1987), *The Philosophy of Welfare, Selected Writings*, Allen & Unwin.

Mellström, Carl and Johannesson, Magnus (2008), Crowding Out In Blood Donation: Was Titmuss Right?, *Journal of the European Economic Association*, Vol. 6, Issue 4, June, 845–63.

Gneezy, Uri and Rustichini, Aldo (2000), A Fine Is a Price, *Journal of Legal Studies*, January, 1–17.

Goldstein, Noah J., Cialdini, Robert B. and Griskevicius, Vladas (2008), A Room With a Viewpoint: Using Social Norms to Motivate Environmental Conservation in Hotels, *Journal of Consumer Research*, Vol. 35, No. 3 (October), 472–82.

Ruff, C. C., Ugazio, G. and Fehr, E. (2013), Changing Social Norm Compliance with Noninvasive Brain Stimulation, *Science*, Vol. 342 (October), 482–4.

Desilver, Drew (2014), Voter Turnout Always Drops off for Midterm Elections, But Why?, Pew Research Center Report, http://www.pewresearch.org/facttank/2014/07/24/voter-turnout-always-drops-off-for-midterm-elections-but-why/, date accessed 2 November 2014.

Funk, Patricia (2010), Social Incentives and Voter Turnout: Evidence from the Swiss Mail Ballot System, *Journal of the European Economic Association*, 8 (5), 1077–1103.

Spector, Mike (2007), The Economics of Hybrids, *Wall Street Journal*, 29 October.

NHTSA (National Highway Traffic Safety Administration) press release (2009), Cash for Clunkers Wraps up with Nearly 700,000 Car Sales and Increased Fuel Efficiency, U.S. Transportation Secretary LaHood Declares Program "Wildly Successful", 26 August.

Simon, Stephanie (2010), The Secret to Turning Consumers Green, *Wall Street Journal*, 18 October.

Beacon Hill Institute Report (2012), Two Years of the Washington, D.C. Bag Tax: An Analysis, August, 1–13.

Nolan, Jessica M., Schultz, Wesley P., Cialdini, Robert B., Goldstein, Noah J. and Griskevicius, Vladas (2008), Normative Social Influence is Underdetected, *Personality and Social Psychology Bulletin*, Vol. 34, No. 7, 913–23.

Allcott, Hunt and Mullainathan, Sendhil (2010), Behavior and Energy Policy, *Science*, Vol. 327, March, 1204–5.

URLs for Southwest Florida Water Management District "Skip a Week" Television Commercials, http://www.youtube.com/watch?v=P-5Jf3Kaa0Q; http://www. youtube.com/watch?v=gdftnNVC6Gg; http://www.swfwmd.state.fl.us/ conservation/ads/, date accessed 2 November 2014.

Southwest Florida Water Management District 2009-2010 "Skip a Week" Campaign Summary, https://www.swfwmd.state.fl.us/files/database/social_research/37/ Social_Marketing_Skip_A_Week_Final_Summary_PDF.pdf, date accessed 2 November 2014.

Frey, B. S. and Oberholzer-Gee, F. (1997), The Cost of Price Incentives: An Empirical Analysis of Motivation Crowding-Out, *American Economic Review*, 87 (4), 746–55.

Kahan, D. M. (2003), The Logic of Reciprocity: Trust, Collective Action, and Law, *Michigan Law Review*, 102 (1), 71–103.

Banerjee, Abhijit V. and Duflo, Esther, *Poor Economics: A Radical Rethinking of the Way to Fight Global Poverty*, PublicAffairs.

Fiszbein, Ariel and Schady, Norbert (2009), Conditional Cash Transfers: Reducing Present and Future Poverty, World Bank Policy Research Report.

Lomelí, Enrique Valencia (2008), Conditional Cash Transfer Programs: Achievements and Illusions, Global Social Policy, Vol. 9 (2), 167–71.

Chapter 10

Thomas, Manoj (2014), Osram Sylvania Case Study, Cornell University.

Keeney, Ralph L. (2012), Value-Focused Brainstorming, Decision Analysis, Vol. 9 (4), 303–13.

Kotler, Philip and Keller, Kevin Lane (2006), *Marketing Management*, Prentice Hall.

Gupta, Sunil and Lehmann, Donald R. (2005), *Managing Customers as Investments: The Strategic Value of Customers in the Long Run*, Pearson Education/Wharton School Publishing.

Kerin, Roger and Peterson, Robert (2012), *Strategic Marketing Problems*, Prentice Hall.

Knowledge @ Wharton (2014), Finding a Place for Market Research in a Big-Data, TechEnabled World, 29 January.

Index

CPSIA information can be obtained
at www.ICGtesting.com
Printed in the USA
LVHW111623260120
644829LV00001B/1